'*A Special Kind of Grief* is a book that would be perfect for any teacher, SENCO or professional working with pupils with SEND or without. As Sarah quite rightly points out, we live in a society where death is treated with fear; a "stiff upper lip" and a hope that we will never have to have difficult conversations with such a vulnerable group (children). What I took from this book, however, is that it is OK to have tricky conversations and to show feelings that we may have otherwise bottled up "for the sake of the children". Sarah's guidance on writing a policy, how to support pupils, families and staff and how to report to the wider community is very clear and well thought out. An essential book for every school.'

– *Kitty Eve, SENCO at Chandag Junior School*

by the same author

Remembering Lucy
ISBN 978 1 78592 307 4
eISBN 978 1 78450 614 8

of related interest

I Have a Question about Death
A Book for Children with Autism Spectrum Disorder or Other Special Needs
Arlen Grad Gaines and Meredith Englander Polsky
ISBN 978 1 78592 750 8
eISBN 978 1 78450 545 5

Helping Children and Adolescents Think
about Death, Dying and Bereavement
Marian Carter
ISBN 978 1 78592 011 0
eISBN 978 1 78450 255 3

Responding to Loss and Bereavement in Schools
A Training Resource to Assess, Evaluate and Improve the School Response
John Holland
ISBN 978 1 84905 692 2
eISBN 978 1 78450 229 4

Supporting People with Intellectual Disabilities
Experiencing Loss and Bereavement
Theory and Compassionate Practice
Edited by Sue Read
ISBN 978 1 84905 369 3
eISBN 978 0 85700 726 1

How People with Autism Grieve, and How to Help
An Insider Handbook
Deborah Lipsky
ISBN 978 1 84905 954 1
eISBN 978 0 85700 789 6

A Special Kind of Grief

The Complete Guide for Supporting
Bereavement and Loss in Special
Schools (and Other SEND Settings)

Sarah Helton

Jessica Kingsley *Publishers*
London and Philadelphia

Every effort has been made to trace copyright holders and to
obtain their permission for the use of copyright material. The
author and the publisher apologize for any omissions and would
be grateful if notified of any acknowledgements that should be
incorporated in future reprints or editions of this book.

Quote on page 23 is reproduced with permission from *A Grief
Observed* by C.S. Lewis © copyright CS Lewis Pte Ltd 1961.

First published in 2017
by Jessica Kingsley Publishers
73 Collier Street
London N1 9BE, UK
and
400 Market Street, Suite 400
Philadelphia, PA 19106, USA

www.jkp.com

Copyright © Sarah Helton 2017

Front cover image source: Anna Novy (taken from *Remembering Lucy*).

Library of Congress Cataloging in Publication Data
A CIP catalog record for this book is available from the Library of Congress

British Library Cataloguing in Publication Data
A CIP catalogue record for this book is available from the British Library

ISBN 978 1 78592 273 2
eISBN 978 1 78450 566 0

Printed and bound in Great Britain

During my teaching career there have been many children whose lives sadly ended too soon. This book is dedicated to them. Each and every one of you has a very special place in my heart.

Acknowledgements

I would like to acknowledge all of the wonderful schools that I have had the honour of working at. I learnt so much from the pupils, families and staff of each of these schools.

- Project AIM, Auburn University, Auburn, Alabama, USA
- Minehead First School, Minehead, Somerset
- Royal United Hospital School, Bath, Somerset
- Charter Primary School, Chippenham, Wiltshire
- St. Nicholas Special School, Chippenham, Wiltshire
- Warmley Park Special School, Warmley, Bristol
- Fiveways Special School, Yeovil, Somerset

Notes

Please note:

- Although the terms 'child', 'pupil' and 'student' have been used throughout this book, please read this as 'any individual with SEND' (SEND stands for special educational needs and disability).
- Although the term 'school' has been used throughout this book, this refers to any community or setting that supports individuals with SEND.

Contents

Introduction

CHAPTER 1

Who Is This Book For?

This book has been written for special schools and schools, colleges and educational establishments that work with children and adults with special educational needs and disability (hereafter abbreviated as SEND). This book will also be beneficial for parents with a child with SEND or anyone who works with, supports, or knows a person with SEND.

I am a SEND teacher with over 20 years of experience working in a wide range of schools (both special and mainstream schools) and other special education organisations.

Sadly, during my career I have experienced the death of many pupils and witnessed the effect that each death has had on the other children (as well as the staff and the wider school community). I have also seen pupils struggle with the death of family members and friends, as well as grief associated with loss (such as through divorce, moving house, a pet dying, friends relocating and changing school). I feel very strongly that children's grief (whatever form that it takes) must never be overlooked.

I have written this book to provide special schools, and other professionals who work with individuals with SEND, with practical information, knowledge and resources so they are fully prepared for whatever form of grief their students experience, whether that is the tragedy of a pupil's death, which affects the entire school community, or children's individual experiences of bereavement and loss. This book hopes to ensure that no child, regardless of their level of need, is left coping alone with grief.

CHAPTER 2

Why Is There a Need
for This Book?

Early in my teaching career I witnessed the devastating impact of a pupil's death on that child's classmates and the school as a whole. I quickly realised that there was very little support and guidance on how best to support children with SEND with grief. At times the grief of these children was either ignored or not fully acknowledged, with staff not knowing how to deal with the difficult situation.

Death is a certainty for us all and although we may not wish to think about it, we all experience death and we all experience other forms of loss (such as the loss from a close friend moving far away or the loss of a relationship through divorce or separation). Most children are fortunate in that their first experience of death doesn't normally occur until they are older, maybe as a teenager with the death of a grandparent. Children with SEND often experience death at a much younger age due to the nature of the medical conditions that some children in special education have.

When working in severe learning difficulties (SLD), profound and multiple learning difficulties (PMLD) and complex needs (CN) special schools I experienced (on average) the death of one pupil a year.

Consider for a moment that if a child joins a special school aged four, by the time s/he leaves aged 16, there could well have been as many as 12 children die in that school.

S/he may not have known all of those children well, but the impact of those deaths will be immense. How many of us experienced 12 deaths by the time we were 16? And this doesn't take into consideration any deaths that may occur outside of the school environment.

UK educational statistics show that up to 70 per cent of schools have at least one bereaved pupil on roll at any one time (Holland,

1993). In one survey 78 per cent of 11–16-year-olds said that they had been bereaved of a close relative or friend (Harrison and Harrington, 2001). By the age of 16, 1 in 20 young people will have experienced the death of one or both of their parents (Parsons, 2011).

At the time of writing this book there was no specific data available that showed the number of bereaved pupils in special schools. My personal experiences and research indicate that all special schools will have at least one bereaved pupil on roll every day of every school year. This includes pupils who are bereaved due to the death of family members, as well as those who have experienced the death of a classmate or friend at school. Following the death of a pupil, there will often be periods of time where whole classes and even the entire school community are grieving.

I passionately believe that *all* children need to be well supported with their grief and although this support could be better for all young people, it most definitely needs to be improved for children with SEND. Children with SEND are more likely to be affected by grief at a younger age and in greater frequency than 'typically developing children'. This, combined with the understanding and communication difficulties that SEND children have, only strengthens the importance of them having good bereavement education and support.

So, are death, bereavement, loss and grief part of your school curriculum and culture? If not, ask yourself why. I'm sure it is not due to a lack of need. Is it instead more to do with a lack of training? Or a lack of awareness of its importance? Or do staff not want to acknowledge that children with SEND experience grief (because they don't truly understand and value the children's emotions and loss)? Or could it be due to staff personally being unable to handle and discuss death and other forms of loss?

Even in our so-called enlightened 21st century, death is a much-ignored subject, especially in western countries. Also, many adults have reservations about discussing any emotionally challenging situations with children, as they fear that they may make the situation worse.

Lee Scott's report, *SEND: The Schools and Colleges Experience. A report to the Secretary of State for Education* (Department for Education, 2016), noted the need for teachers to be better trained in the issues of loss, trauma and separation. It highlighted 'the general lack of knowledge that teaching staff, including SENCOs [special educational needs coordinators], have of child development and the impact of trauma, loss and separation' (p.8). It also noted that 'It's important that staff have access to training, and that leaders both allow and encourage staff to undertake training to improve awareness and expertise in SEND, and the impact of loss and trauma on a child's ability to learn' (p.9).

This need for better staff training and in turn better support of bereaved and grieving children is not only shown in this report, it is also borne out in classrooms across the country.

Sadly, I am sure that every teacher will encounter the issue of a pupil death or the death of a pupil's close relative at some point during their career. And a special school teacher will unfortunately encounter pupil deaths with much greater frequency. So we need to be prepared for such tragic occurrences, as well as more general issues of loss and grief, by being well informed and well equipped with knowledge and resources. This will allow us to very effectively support and care for our pupils during the grieving process (whatever the reason for their grief) and in turn enable us to cope personally and professionally with the issues that surround death, bereavement, grief and loss.

CHAPTER 3

The Importance of
Acknowledging Grief

It is well known and has been proved by countless psychiatrists, psychologists and counsellors that ignoring grief and trying to paper over the cracks that loss brings to our lives will ultimately lead to emotional and possibly psychological problems. This doesn't just apply to adults, it is relevant at any age, whether you are a child or an adult.

> Some may start to grieve, but get stuck. The early sense of shock and disbelief just goes on and on. Years may pass and still the sufferer finds it hard to believe that the person they loved is dead. Others may carry on being unable to think of anything else… Occasionally, the depression that occurs with every bereavement may deepen to the extent that food and drink are refused and thoughts of suicide arise. (Royal College of Psychiatrists, 2015)

Death is a subject avoided by most people, especially with children. Most adults are perplexed by what to say to another adult who is mourning, but when a child is bereaved they often try to avoid having a conversation about the loss and ignore the issue and all questions about death. This avoidance of the issue also tends to apply to other forms of grief.

It is our natural instinct to protect children, but trying to protect them from death and the emotions of grief is unwise and unhelpful.

All children, regardless of their background, race, gender, ability or disabilities, have the right to have their grief acknowledged and be given the support, time and opportunities to express their thoughts, feelings and emotions.

Children who have SEND may communicate their grief differently, but grief is grief, and their grief is just as valid and powerful as anyone else's and must never be overlooked, ignored or forgotten. Doing so will only leave them in a greater state of confusion and, just like anyone whose grief is neglected, this could impact on their emotional and psychological health beyond all measure.

This book explains how we can all support children with SEND with their grief.

You do not need to be an educational psychologist, psychiatrist or counsellor to help children manage their grief. In most circumstances, a kind and understanding person who is there for the child is all the 'training' that is required.

In exceptional circumstances, you may need to refer a child to another professional (see Chapter 16 for further information).

CHAPTER 4

The School

An Overview of School Policies and Procedures

Educators are in a unique position to help bereaved and grieving children and young people. Schools are often the one constant that children and young people have in their lives.

Like people, schools will probably want to ignore the possibility of their school being affected by a death, especially the death of a pupil. But a school that has prepared for these eventualities will be in a much better position to handle the tragic event if it occurs and in turn better support the pupils, staff and the wider community with the loss.

When a death or other form of loss occurs, the school needs to have plans, procedures and resources immediately at hand so that staff know exactly what to do and don't have to scrabble around to put things together at a time when emotions are high.

Detailed preparation is, therefore, required. You do not want to be asking these questions in the middle of a bereavement or traumatic event:

- Has a policy been written?
- Are procedures fully developed for implementing the policy?
- Are these procedures written down?
- Is everyone aware of the policy and procedures?
- Does everyone know what their roles are in carrying out the procedures?

Schools need to have the following in place:

- An emergency response plan (that covers all forms of emergency: weather disruption, vandalism, fire, IT failure, death, etc. – this document is normally devised by the local authority).

- A bereavement and loss policy.

- Detailed procedures and plans for what to do when a death occurs. This means plans for day one – informing staff, pupils and the wider community – onwards. What should happen in school during the first week following the death, how to communicate with the bereaved family, who will attend the funeral and thoughts and ideas on how to hold a memorial service at school.

- Detailed procedures and plans for what to do when an individual child experiences a loss.

- Defined roles for implementing the procedures and plans.

- A curriculum that teaches the concepts of life, death and loss.

- A curriculum that explores the emotions and feelings that surround someone dying, as well as those associated with experiencing other forms of grief and loss.

Think about whether you have these policies and procedures in place in your school. If you do, have a look through them as you read this book to check that you have everything completely covered. If you don't have these things in place, don't worry – each of these areas will be addressed in depth in later sections of this book.

A Death Occurs

CHAPTER 5

How to Inform Staff

Never underestimate the immense impact that the death of a pupil (or member of staff or anyone close to the school) will have on a school community.

Once you have been informed of the death of a pupil, member of staff or person close to the school community it is vital that the school has a clear plan to follow. The coming days, weeks and months are going to be difficult enough without the hindrance of miscommunication. Ensure you have a plan for disseminating the information and stick to it – to the letter.

The person who has died may have been unwell so there could have been some indication that this death was imminent, but in my experience even if you are aware of the likelihood of the death, you never fully believe it's actually going to happen, especially if it is a pupil. Consequently, there will undoubtedly be shock in the school.

When people learn of a death, they want information. If this isn't given to them in a timely fashion, they seek the information out in a range of less appropriate places (including social media) and this means that they run the risk of gaining inaccurate information.

As the employer, it is key that you share the right level of information with all the appropriate people at the right time and in the right manner. Otherwise, inaccurate and potentially damaging information will be shared and possibly spread further. Even if you cannot provide all of the details regarding the death, give people the accurate information that you do have. Omissions and half-truths only lead to anxieties and gossiping and, in turn, negatively impact on the school at a time when it is already in a difficult and vulnerable position.

Understandably, the death of a student has a particularly huge impact on the entire school community – we do not expect or prepare ourselves for the fact that children may die. Some pupils and staff will be affected more than others, but the death and loss needs to be acknowledged by the whole community.

When telling staff members of a death, it is normal that some staff will be unwilling to acknowledge the loss in public. They may also be unwilling to discuss the death and may feel that the children shouldn't be exposed to it either. These feelings are generally as a result of the staff member's own personal experience of previous bereavements and/or their lack of understanding and knowledge concerning grief. They may want to ignore the issue, feeling this is the best thing to do for themselves and the children, as they falsely believe that talking about the bereavement will create further upset.

'It is essential that the school is led by a strong leadership team, with senior leaders modelling 'appropriate grief' (more on 'appropriate grief' in Chapter 6), and who are around school, present and available to staff. Staff should be educated on the importance of supporting students' grief. Staff need to understand the details of the death and be capable of answering students' questions and supporting them throughout the bereavement process.

Telling staff

When informing staff of a death, endeavour to get all the staff together and tell them at the same time. If you are unable to do this, ensure everyone in the building is told as quickly as possible and in person. Staff who are off-site should be telephoned so they are aware, too.

When informing staff of the death it will be helpful for you to do the following things.

- Most importantly, only provide information that the parents/carers/family are happy for you to share. Typically, the following would be shared with staff:
  - When the death occurred.
  - The circumstances of the death (e.g. they died due to complications associated with pneumonia or had an epileptic seizure).
  - Where the death occurred (e.g. at home, a hospital or a hospice).

- Any wishes that the parents/carers/family have shared to date (e.g. no flowers to be sent to the house, or the funeral is planned for the following week but the exact date is still to be confirmed).

- When the news should be shared with pupils.

• You also need to reiterate to staff that the school's bereavement and loss policy and procedures must be followed. Give them a brief overview of the policy and procedures and remind staff where they can find them.

• Make sure staff know what support mechanisms are available to both them and the pupils and how these can be accessed.

• Schedule a short meeting for the end of the day so that you can check in with staff and see how they and the pupils are coping with the news. At this meeting you should also go through the bereavement and loss policy and procedures with specific reference to what will take place in the coming days. It is good to remind staff what to expect in terms of their own emotions, as well as what feelings and behaviours they might expect to see in pupils (but remember to keep this meeting very brief – staff have only just received this difficult news and they need time to process and reflect on the death).

Following the death of a pupil (or anyone close to the school), staff may feel:

• that they are operating on autopilot

• emotionally detached

• numb

• anxious

• depressed

• angry

• sad

• irritable

• concerned about doing and/or saying the right thing

• that it is hard to concentrate

- as if they are on the edge
- a sense of guilt.

They may also experience physical symptoms such as:

- headaches
- stomach aches
- lack of appetite
- insomnia.

During the initial meeting with staff, as well as going through the emotions, feelings and symptoms they may experience, emphasise that these are all normal grief responses. It is also useful to share with staff the different tasks of mourning (shown below). Be sure to stress that it isn't as simple as moving neatly from one task to another; instead the pattern of grief is unique to each individual. However, if staff know what they and the pupils are likely to feel, this generally makes the process easier.

The Four Tasks of Mourning

In his book *Grief Counseling and Grief Therapy* (2008) William Worden suggests that there are 'Four Tasks of Mourning':

1. To accept the reality of the loss.

2. To process the pain of grief.

3. To adjust to a world without the deceased.

4. To find an enduring connection with the deceased in the midst of embarking on a new life.

   No one ever told me that grief felt so like fear. I am not afraid, but the sensation is like being afraid. The same fluttering in the stomach, the same restlessness, the yawning, I keep on swallowing. At other times it feels like being mildly drunk or concussed. There is a sort of invisible blanket between the world and me. I find it hard to take in what anyone says… Yet I want the others to be about me. (Lewis, 1961)

As school leaders, it is crucial to underscore to staff that if they need to talk, have some time out, etc., there is always someone available to listen. It is, therefore, important that you name who this person is, as well as provide information about how to contact them.

In the initial days after the death, it is useful to have an extra member of staff available who can fill in when a member of staff needs a short break away from their duties in class.

It is also advisable to have a space designated for 'staff time out' – a place where they can go to get away from the demands of class, to be quiet and reflect or to talk to someone else. (A similar place should also be made available for pupils – more on this in Chapter 11.)

Supporting bereaved children can be a very stressful job. It is, therefore, important for staff to look after themselves and understand how they are personally coping with the loss so that they, in turn, can support the children they work with to the best of their abilities.

It is also vital for staff to know their own limitations. Do not offer to do more than you are capable of doing. There are always other members of staff you can ask to help. Don't feel you have to do everything and be there for everyone. If you overstretch yourself, you could end up letting down a grieving child or a grieving member of staff, because you will not be there for them when you are no longer able to cope. Also, doing more than you are able to do will ultimately negatively affect your emotional and physical self.

Finally, it is much easier to support grieving children if you are informed and knowledgeable about how children are likely to react and behave following a death. (These areas will be discussed in Chapters 9 and 10.)

CHAPTER 6

How to Tell Pupils

Children aren't born with a fear of death; it is something that is passed on to them from adults and society as they grow up. Listening and showing that you care are the key aspects of supporting a bereaved child.

This chapter looks at how to tell a group of pupils about a death, for example a death that affects the entire school community, as well as how to tell individual children of a loss.

Staff need to tell pupils of the death in accordance with the school's bereavement and loss policy and in the manner and time that has been decided by the school leadership team. It is generally wise for all classes to be informed by their own teacher and at roughly the same time. This way you avoid children hearing of the death from other pupils on the playground or around the school. The longer you leave sharing the news, the more chance they have of getting the wrong information and being unsupported.

The start of a school day or the beginning of a session are generally the best times to tell children and the information needs to be shared in a very inclusive, gentle and warm manner. A session such as circle time would be ideal. As the teacher, you will know how well the children in your class knew the child/person who has died, and this will help you gauge how to share the news and help to determine the level of grief that they may experience. But remember, we can never really know how someone will react. If the person who has died was a child or member of staff who was in your class, telling the children in this class will be the most difficult.

When talking to children about the death and their grief, remember that a child's attention span is related to the amount of information they can grasp at any particular time. When they hit their limit, they may switch from emotions that seem appropriate to those that seem inappropriate, for example laughing uncontrollably.

This behaviour allows them to bypass talking about the death. This technique is normal and provides a safety mechanism for the child so that they don't become emotionally overwhelmed.

When telling the children about a death you need to be as concrete as possible with your language. Do not speak in euphemisms, for example 'They have gone away' or 'They are sleeping.' This will be confusing for children (especially those with SEND) and could lead to them believing that the person will come back one day. Provide information in short, simple sentences. Having brief (more frequent) conversations about the death is better than one big, long talk. Telling them about the death isn't a one-off event: our children need to have the information repeated (possibly many times) for them to really understand the loss and know that it is permanent.

Preparing to share the news with pupils

Be well prepared for the discussion. Have a photo of the child/person who has died to show the class, so that it is absolutely clear to them who you are talking about.

Think about the language you are going to use in advance. If it is appropriate to use verbal language ensure that you speak in short, simple sentences and at the child's receptive language level. Ensure you use the real words of: dead, death, died and so on.

Remember, do not speak in euphemisms.

As adults, we tend to use a great many euphemisms – descriptive phrases such as 'passed on', 'gone to the other side', 'in heaven' and so on – to express death, rather than just using the simple and very accurate words of death and dead. We must ensure that we never confuse and complicate things for our children by using euphemisms.

Generally, the greatest difficulty in telling children with SEND of a death (and then supporting them with the bereavement) is around communication. How do we communicate the information to them?

We cannot rely on spoken communication alone.

It is imperative that we come up with a wealth of different modes of communication that will convey the information and, in turn, allow the child to express their emotions and thoughts. Use the modes of communication that are appropriate to your children (e.g. sign language, symbols, photos, objects of reference, pictures, communication aids, switches, Eye Gaze, etc.). Just as you must think about and prepare the verbal language to use, make sure you also have all of these Augmentative and Alternative Communication (AAC) resources and equipment prepared.

You need to ensure that you have the means to communicate the following words and concepts:

• dead

• alive (so that you can compare 'dead' and 'alive' and explain each)

• will not see them again

• sad

• angry

• upset.

You also need to communicate words that explain how and why they died (to the appropriate level of detail for the children), such as:

• unwell

• accident

• in hospital

• at home.

Children want and look for the truth surrounding a death as much as adults. It is imperative that this is given to them (again, to the level of their developmental understanding).

Ways to explain death

Here are some examples of words that you could use when explaining death to a child.

• When a person dies, they stop living. A dead person does not breathe, see or hear. They cannot do things. Their body[1] has

---

1   Check that the child understands that the word body means the whole person – the whole body. Often we talk about the head and the body being two separate things so a child may interpret 'their body has completely stopped working' as meaning their head is still OK.

completely stopped working. The person who has died has gone forever.

- When someone we like dies, we can have many different feelings. We can feel angry, sad and lonely. With time, these feelings start to go away. We are able to learn to live without the person. The person is not forgotten. We remember them and the time we spent together.

Informing an individual child of a death or a loss

It is very rare that a teaching professional will be the first person to inform a child of the death of someone close to them (such as a parent or sibling) or a loss (such as a parents divorcing or the fact that they are moving to another country); it is most likely that this will be done by a family member. Here is some advice and guidance in case this situation does occur.

- Make sure that the member of staff sharing the news is someone that the child has a very strong and positive connection with.

- Tell the child away from their class group, as the other children will not be aware of the sad news that is being imparted to their friend and their activity could be very distracting and incongruous to the news. At a later time you will need to explain to the rest of the class that their friend may be sad as they have [explain what has happened].

- Inform the child in a place where they will feel very relaxed and comfortable, such as the library or sensory garden, that will also be a safe place if they take the news very badly (they may feel happiest and most relaxed in the hydrotherapy pool, but this could be a very unsafe environment for them to be in when hearing the news). Also, being given sad news in such a special place may make it difficult for them to really enjoy it again in the future.

- Be in a place where you are able to call for help and support if it is required.

- Prepare the necessary symbols and resources to communicate the information to the child and that allow them to ask questions.

- Have tissues, wipes, a drink and so on prepared for the child.

- If the child has certain medical conditions that could be affected by hearing the bad news, such as asthma, epilepsy or heart or breathing difficulties, be prepared with any possible necessary medical interventions.

It is most likely that a family member will impart the initial news of a death and that you will need to reiterate the information to the child in the days and weeks that follow. You should follow the steps above as you go through retelling and explaining the news to the child.

You will then need to continue to support the bereaved child as described in the rest of this chapter.

Ways to support a bereaved child

Like bereaved adults, bereaved children need to work through the Four Tasks of Mourning (which were discussed in Chapter 5). The following suggestions will assist this process of mourning.

- With the child, look at photos and videos of the person who has died. By doing this you help to facilitate and support the child's expression of sadness and anger. As they express these emotions, reinforce what they are feeling and why. Use symbols and all relevant AAC to support this (as below).

  - When they are angry, show them the symbol/picture/sign (whatever their preferred mode of communication is) for 'angry', 'dead', 'OK' and 'miss', along with a photo of the child who has died as you say, 'You are angry because David is dead. It's OK to be angry. You miss David.'

  - When they are crying or sad, follow the same approach. Show them the symbol/picture/sign (whatever their preferred mode of communication is) for 'sad', 'dead', 'OK', 'miss' and 'crying', along with a photo of the child who has died as you say, 'You are sad, because David is dead. It's OK to be sad and crying. You miss David.'

- Read storybooks about death and loss, such as my children's storybook, *Remembering Lucy*, about grief and bereavement in a special school. (See Appendix E for a list of useful books and resources about bereavement and loss to use with children with SEND.)

- Display 'appropriate grief'. In other words do not hide your own sadness and tears from the students. They will only truly understand what grieving is and how to manage it if they see others doing it, so be a good grief role model. As you feel sad, show this to the children and explain why you are feeling this way. Use symbols and all relevant AAC to support this, for example when you are feeling sad, let the children see your sad face and also show them a photo of the person who has died and the symbol/picture/sign for 'sad', 'dead' or 'miss' as you say, 'I am feeling sad because that song reminded me of David. David is dead and I miss David. Let's sing the song again and think about how much David loved it. That will make me smile.' You, of course, do not want to be out of control with your own grief in front of the children, but the children do need to *see* grief to be able to start understanding it and to be able to grieve themselves. Reassure the children that your feelings are natural and that you are OK.

- Provide the child with safe activities and opportunities to express their grief (e.g. painting, play dough, using construction kits and physical tasks such as shredding paper or throwing balls). Reassure them that all feelings are OK and acceptable. Expressing their emotions through these activities will be very cathartic for them.

- Having a comforting object to hold can be a great support for children. This object can be whatever is an important and comforting item for the child. It could be a toy, a blanket, a cushion, etc. Having access to this object can help children get through particularly sad and angry times (more on this in Chapter 11).

Key things bereaved children need
Bereaved children need:

- to have their questions answered

- help to understand about the death

- to be given the opportunity to be involved, for example in the funeral, memorial service or special assembly at school (more on this in Chapters 13 and 22)

- to be given security, affection and extra reassurance
- opportunities to talk in their own time
- opportunities to be left alone
- to know that they are safe and that there are people who care for them
- the ability to talk to others (including other professionals) if needed
- ways to remember the person.

> Nothing impacts a child more than the death of someone close to them or someone they loved. It really is fantasy to believe that children will merely 'get over' a bereavement, that they are simply 'too young' to be truly affected by the loss or that they don't have the understanding to process what has happened.

Accept all feelings

It is vital that adults let children know that all of their feelings will be accepted. We need to ensure that children are given permission to grieve as well as having appropriate and healthy opportunities (times and places) to express their grief. This will enable them to cope and grow through the loss, as well as to handle the transitions that it presents in their lives. We never want a child to hide their feelings or feel embarrassed or ashamed of them. We must strive to foster an environment in which the child feels able to ask questions and knows that their emotions are not going to be ignored or belittled.

Just as with an adult, things that are unresolved or left unsaid grow and become a bigger issue. As adults and as professionals working with children, it is our duty to support them through the grieving process and to answer their questions. A child with verbal language may ask things such as:

- Are you going to die, too?
- Will I die?
- Why did Lucy have to die?
- Did it hurt?

You need to answer these questions honestly.

Non-verbal children

But what about children who are non-verbal? They may not have the ability to ask the questions above, but it doesn't mean that they aren't thinking and feeling them.

So we have to reassure children who are without verbal language that they are safe. Reassure them that their family, you, other staff members, friends and so on are alive and here for them.

Providing children with a sense of security is crucial after a loss, and with children who are non-verbal you need to do this with your words, your actions, your emotions and your closeness (your physical and emotional closeness).

You may be unsure as to how much a child who is severely disabled and/or non-verbal understands about a death, but even at the most basic level they will know that the person is no longer present; they may even try to seek them out. These children will see and feel this loss just as any other child does and they will need guidance, care and love to come to terms with this loss. The person who has died may have been the child who they laid beside to do their physiotherapy exercises each day, so they will feel this loss each morning. The child's face will no longer be lying next to them making them giggle and the hand that they always held to practise rocking from side to side will no longer be there. These changes will all be seen and felt by the child and therefore cannot be overlooked, especially as they may be understanding and experiencing far more than we appreciate.

Never underestimate the extent to which they may experience the loss.

We must also remember that it is impossible *not to communicate with children*. Even if a child is non-verbal, they will pick up on the mood of the school/classroom/house. They will feel the emotional changes following a death (such as people's moods being different and the energy and activity of the class changing). They will also see physical changes in the environment (such as less furniture, wheelchairs and physiotherapy equipment missing from the room and certain noises and smells no longer being present), along with changes in people's behaviour (such as crying, sadness or perhaps not wanting to eat). All of this is communication and whatever the individual's cognitive ability, they will pick up on these changes. So reassurance and care are needed to support them through these changes and through their grief.

If you respond to a grieving child in a caring, sensitive and developmentally appropriate manner, you will help to normalise their difficult emotions and concerns. Answering their questions will also help to reassure them that they are safe and help with the long-term grieving process.

It's not just about the current death

We also need to remember that although a current death may not affect a child, it could bring back feelings from a previous loss. Past bereavements can be triggered by any number of things, not just the news of a new death; it could be a song, a person, a place or a certain activity – the list is endless.

Always accept any loss that the child has experienced and always acknowledge the effects of that grief at any time. To ignore their loss suggests that they and the situation are unimportant; it can also contribute to removing any existence of the person who has died.

> We must bear in mind that there is no set timeline to the pattern of grief. Instead, it is a lifelong process; at different points in our lives the impact of a death can be reawakened and there will be a need to work through the loss again.

To summarise

Adults tend to want to protect children from the issues of death and dying and this can be even more prevalent with children with SEND. It is also often assumed that children do not have the ability to understand death. Although to a certain extent this may be the case for some children with SEND, we tend to miscalculate their awareness of death and loss. In fact, we often tend to underestimate their strength and skills in being able to handle difficult aspects of life.

The challenge for the adult is to find different ways to communicate the loss, as words may not always be appropriate. Use all modes of communication relevant to the child – verbal, visual and all other sensory modes that apply – and do not neglect the power and communication of closeness – being with the child to help communicate the loss and to comfort them. And even if the child does have verbal skills, they do not necessarily have the words to express fully their sadness and loss, so their behaviour will communicate their grief instead.

Children (including children with SEND) do not need to be sheltered from the emotions and feelings of death. Instead, they require guidance and reassurance on how to express their often overwhelming and powerful feelings, thoughts and emotions. Children can grieve as intensely as adults, but often it is in a slightly different manner.

Another challenge is providing a wealth and breadth of activities within which they can work through their loss and express their emotions and thoughts. Be open to the child communicating their grief in a plethora of ways; not merely words or emotional outbursts, but also through artwork, stories, role-play and so on.

Until now, bereavement resources for children with SEND have been rather limited, but this book hopes to address that, giving you everything you need in this one resource.

In Chapter 11 you will find a wide range of activity and resource ideas to support grieving children. However, never forget that you are in fact the child's greatest resource as you know them and you know how to listen to them and how to 'talk' to them. Your connection with the child is by far the greatest resource in supporting their bereavement. This book merely gives you ideas to support that connection.

CHAPTER 7

How to Let Parents, Families and the Wider Community Know

How you communicate the death of a member of the school community to parents, families and the wider community must follow the wishes of the family of the deceased. Once you are clear on what they are happy for you to share, you can then follow the communication guidance contained in your bereavement and loss policy (more on this in Chapter 28 and Appendix A).

Typically, you will write a letter for parents (on the day you are informed of the death or the first school day after this) that will be sent home with each pupil. This letter will provide basic details of the death and outline the support that is being provided to students, as well as give information to parents/carers/families as to what they can do at home to help the child. (A template for this letter is included in Appendix B.)

Where possible and appropriate, share this letter with the family of the child or person who has died before it gets shared with the school community.

There will probably be some families in your school that are more vulnerable to the news of a pupil death than others, for example, families whose daughter/son was close friends with the child who has died or families where their own child may currently be very ill in hospital. It is advisable to identify these vulnerable parents/carers/families and give them a personal phone call to let them know of the death.

If the bereavement affects a particular class or cohort in the school, the parents of these children will require a more detailed letter, explaining the implications for the class, what extra support will be available to them and so on.

Staff who are not in school on the day you learn of the death should be telephoned so that they are aware of the news prior to coming back into school. Also, professionals who regularly come into school, such as speech therapists, physiotherapists and so on, should be informed (ideally by telephone but if necessary via email) so that when they next come into school they do not inadvertently say something inappropriate or ask to work with the deceased child.

If your school has a regular newsletter (e.g. weekly or half termly) then a piece should also be written to be included in the next newsletter.

Once the initial letter has been received by all parents, if the death is that of a pupil or member of staff you may wish to include this letter on your school website or provide a brief statement for the website to ensure that all members of the school community are aware of the death. However, remember to ask the family of the deceased individual before sharing such information online.

The rise in the use of social media can mean that some parents and families are aware of the death ahead of the school informing them of it. Even if families have received news of the death in a more informal manner it is still important for the school to share news of the death. This formal announcement will ensure people have accurate details of the death rather than rumours and possible inaccurate information.

Pupils

CHAPTER 8

How Grief Affects Children at Different Ages and Developmental Stages

How grief affects a child depends on a number of factors. First, the developmental and cognitive age of a child will influence the way in which they react to a bereavement. Other influencing factors will be: previous life experiences, the nature of the death, the level of coping strategies that the child has acquired so far in life and the family's beliefs and culture, specifically in relation to death.

When supporting individuals with SEND with bereavement you need to think about the developmental/cognitive age of the person in terms of what they will be able to understand and comprehend. You also have to take into consideration their receptive and expressive communication age when talking to them about the death.

Children's understanding of death at different ages

Children with a cognitive level below 2 years

Before babies are able to talk, they recognise when there are significant changes in their environment. The disappearance of a significant caregiver will be noticed by them and expressed by crying and them trying to seek out the missing person. Children functioning below two years of age will also feel this.

At this stage, children are highly impacted and influenced by the emotions of the adults around them and they do not understand the ramifications of someone dying (i.e. that it is forever).

Children with a cognitive level of 2 to 5 years

At this level, children continue to be highly affected by the emotions of those they are around. They also think about things in a very literal sense. Therefore, we must not use euphemisms such as 'sleeping', 'gone away' and so on, as these can lead to a great many confusions and misunderstandings (euphemisms should be avoided with all children, especially those with SEND). Using such language could lead to the child believing that the person will one day come back.

However, they may have a basic understanding of death, for example when they see a dead badger on the side of the road, they know that it will not get up and run around.

The concept of forever is something that this age group finds very difficult to comprehend. They do not see the permanence of death and their basic understanding of death may result in them having a limited reaction to it.

Children in this age range are egocentric and believe that everything and everyone revolves around them, and this can lead to them thinking that they cause things to occur. Therefore, they may feel that they caused the death to happen. Because children in this age group tend to be very engaged by magic, stories and fairy tales, they may also believe that 'their magical skills' will mean they are able to bring the person back to life.

The grief of children at this level will probably be displayed in short bursts, but it can be intense and can occur at specific times (times related to the person who has died). For example, if they always sat by the child at lunchtime this can be a particularly difficult time of the day for them when their grief is most keenly felt and exhibited.

Children with a cognitive level of two to five years do not yet have a fully formed understanding of death and they may say things like, 'I know Chloe died, but will she be coming to my birthday party?' Be patient, answer their questions and keep gently reiterating that the person has died and will not be coming back and therefore they cannot come to the child's birthday party.

Often children of this developmental age will regress with their skills and behaviours. They may become very clingy, want to be fed (even if they have already acquired the skill of feeding themselves), not want to sleep in their own bed, start wetting the bed and so on.

- Allow the child to regress, and remember this is just part of the grieving process. They haven't lost these skills forever. Think about when you have mourned the loss of someone close to you – you often don't have the energy to wash or cook any food, but you still have the skills to do so.

- Hold the child and give them the extra care, support and attention they require.

- Allow them to express their anger.

- Support the child in play. Have art supplies, toys, dressing-up clothes, etc. that help facilitate the expression of grief.

- Encourage and organise times of fun and happiness.

- Support grieving by modelling your own appropriate patterns of grief. Share your own experiences and stories of grief (within the understanding of their developmental stage) and let them see when you are feeling sad.

- Any specific issues of grief that arise are often best supported in a group situation where the child doesn't have to be the sole focus of attention.

Children with a cognitive level of 6 to 12 years

Children of this age often enjoy fantasy and, as a result, may perceive death as a person that can 'get you' if you do something wrong. If their thoughts are along these lines when someone dear to them dies, they may believe that it has happened because they have done something wrong or bad.

At the higher end of this cognitive age range, children begin to understand that death is final and permanent. They may be enthralled by the physical aspects of dying and the rituals of death and ask lots of questions.

As they mature, they will learn that death is universal, totally unavoidable and inescapable for us all. This in turn can lead to them having deep fears about their own death, such as how it will occur and when.

Children with a cognitive level of 13+ years

At this developmental stage, an understanding of death is in place and it is the effects of grief that are the larger concern. The physiological and emotional challenges of adolescence make grieving even more difficult. At this age, they wish to be treated as independent individuals, so they may hide their grief and not ask for help.

Teenagers (and those functioning at a teenage level) often have very strong ideas and opinions about death and so can challenge the beliefs and explanations of death that are presented to them by others.

Often teens discuss death and dying at great length, but this is normally with their peers rather than their families.

Young adults may deal with the awareness of their own mortality by being involved in risk-taking behaviour.

Table 8.1 Overview of the understanding and typical reactions and behaviours that children have at different developmental ages

Cognitive age	Their understanding	Typical reactions and behaviours
Under 2 years	• No understanding of death	• May try to look for the person who has died • Becoming clingy • Disrupted sleep and feeding patterns • Possibly crying inconsolably
2–5 years	• May see death as reversible • May feel they caused the person to die • Having fantasy thoughts – they may construct fantasies and stories to fill in their gaps of knowledge surrounding the death • May think that they caused the death and/or that they can 'magic' the dead person back • Generally don't understand that death is final and that it is universal (all living things will eventually die)	• Regression of behaviours and skills • Loud and angry outbursts • Sleep difficulties • Unhappy with any changes to their routines • Fear of being separated from their main caregivers • Lots of questions • Anxiety over being left, even for a very short period of time • May become anxious about the dark • May require reassurance that dead people feel no pain • No understanding of the permanence of death

Cognitive age	Their understanding	Typical reactions and behaviours
6–12 years	• Tend to think of death as a 'character' – a shadowy being that can be defeated as long as you know how • Coming to realise that death is permanent • At the top of this age range they normally understand what death means and think about how death can occur and even consider things such as 'Is there an afterlife?'	• May develop an obsession with death and dying • Angry, guilty, sad, withdrawn, depressed, lonely • Possible problems at school • Sleeping difficulties • Nightmares
13+ years	• Know death is permanent	• May lose some of their independence and be more reliant on adults than they were previously • Angry, guilty, sad, withdrawn, depressed, lonely • Insecure, have low self-esteem • May feel rejected • May use jokes and sarcasm as a means of coping • May become involved in risk-taking behaviour

CHAPTER 9

Common Signs of Grieving in Children

Remember that there is no 'normal'. Each child will display their grief in their own time period and in their own individual manner.

The following are the common signs of grieving to be aware of and to look out for in your pupils:

- depression
- being withdrawn
- poor concentration
- complaining of illness (e.g. headaches and stomach aches)
- anxiety
- acting out
- being flighty and unable to listen properly
- being disorganised
- inability to follow instructions
- fear of illness
- impulsive behaviour
- being unsociable
- saying that they want to be with the dead person
- acting like the class clown
- overachieving
- extreme bossiness
- bullying
- being over-talkative

- demonstrating regressive behaviours
- sleeping problems
- eating problems
- regression of skills.

If these symptoms of grieving continue for many months, even with support from school and home (as outlined in the following sections of this book), or escalate, then a referral to another professional may be needed (see Chapter 16 for further information).

CHAPTER 10

Common Behaviours of Grieving Children

There are many things that can impact a child's reactions to death and their associated behaviours, including:

- their chronological, developmental and cognitive age
- the level of attachment they have to the person who has died
- their prior experiences of illness, death and loss
- how the death occurred (long illness, accident, sudden death, suicide, etc.)
- their family's cultural background and religious beliefs
- the support networks they have at home and school
- the gender of the child (boys are less likely to easily show their emotions).

Physical and behavioural reactions to death

Physical reactions

- Tiredness
- Headaches
- Nausea
- Feeling cold
- Shivering
- Minor illnesses
- Loss of appetite
- Panic attacks
- Dry mouth

- Lower activity levels
- Self neglect

Behavioural reactions

- Lack of motivation
- Aggression
- Being unable to concentrate
- Restlessness
- Being disorganised
- Being detached
- Separation anxiety
- Not wanting to go to school

Feelings affect behaviour

It is totally normal for a child to have a very strong reaction to the death of someone close to them. The behaviours that result from this reaction may seem far from normal, but they are indeed typical. This can range from being quiet and distant, to temperamental, disruptive and aggressive. For some children this may include very challenging physical behaviour.

Children who exhibit challenging behaviour need to express their emotions as any other child does, but it is our job to make sure that in doing so they do not hurt themselves or others. In these circumstances you may need to use positive handling plans (such as Team-Teach, PROACT-SCIPr-UK or Positive Handling; for more information see Appendix F) in accordance with the approach and training employed by your school. When the child is calm and receptive to your support you can then talk to them about their grief and support their thoughts and understanding with more positive physical outlets (see Chapter 11).

Being withdrawn is a behaviour that can often be overlooked, especially if the child is without verbal language or doesn't have a very gregarious nature. Being withdrawn doesn't cause others a challenge like a physical behaviour can, so it can easily go unrecognised. For a child with PMLD or a child who is normally more engaged it can be a very strong sign that they are struggling with a bereavement or loss.

Following a bereavement some children can become overly concerned about death and illness. They may spend a lot of time thinking about whether they are now going to die or if their family and friends are going to die. These children will need reassuring that just because one person they know has died, this doesn't mean that everyone around them will now die.

Other less common but possible behaviours that children may exhibit are:

- talking to the person who has died or talking about them in the present tense

- imitating the person who has died: their speech, mannerisms, gestures and so on

- starting to idolise the person who has died

- developing their own individual spiritual beliefs, rituals and practices that are unique to them.

As with any new behaviours that a child displays, these behaviours need to be monitored. If you feel that the behaviours are escalating or remaining for too long (in spite of the support you are giving them), you will need to talk to their parents/carers/family and recommend that further advice and guidance be sought from other professionals (for further information see Chapter 16).

CHAPTER 11

Ways to Support Grieving Children

It is often thought that children can 'bounce back' from things more easily than adults – this is a myth. All individuals (adults and children) grieve in their own way and in their own time. Assuming that children will quickly bounce back from a bereavement is a very dangerous assumption as it means that the child's emotions are unsupported and they are left to cope on their own.

Don't try to suppress a child's grief.

You may wish to protect the child and think that by masking their emotions you are helping them, but by stifling a child's grief you are ultimately causing further problems. All children, regardless of their developmental level, need to work through their grief in their own way and in their own time.

All children will display grief through their behaviours. If children do not have verbal language and therefore lack words to express their grief, their behaviours may be the only way that they can convey their grief.

As long as it is safe to do so, allow children to express their grief in any way they wish. Remember, for children this can include putting all thoughts of the death to one side and getting on with the job of being a child, playing and having some fun. In this way, children have a wonderful safety mechanism – their bodies can only cope with so much emotion at any one time. When they can process no more grief they will have time ignoring the death. During this period, they will be regaining the energy to be able to face things again when it is appropriate and possible for them to do so.

Children dip in and out of grief.

Children need time and space to work through their grief in their own way.

Managing change

For children with SEND, their 'normal world' is bound in structures and routines, and this becomes even more important during a period of grief. A death will undoubtedly result in some changes, but as far as possible these changes need to be managed slowly and sensitively to avoid extra confusion and distress.

The more that things can remain 'normal', the easier it will be for the child to cope.

When children are younger (or are at an earlier developmental stage), they are generally happy with basic explanations and definitions of death, but as they get older, they will probably require greater detail and more answers to their questions.

Answering a child's questions and concerns and the overall support given to grieving children is not just for the weeks and months following the death, it needs to be part of the on-going support and development for the child (and part of the on-going ethos of a school). Like adults, children will re-grieve at different points in their lives, with episodes being triggered by any number of events, large or small.

Understanding death

A child with SEND will find it hard to understand what death really means, especially the fact that it is forever. They may have no understanding of the finality and permanence of death. If they have not developed this awareness, they will often long for things to return to the way they were. For some children, a full understanding of the conclusiveness of death may never be achieved, but this does not mean that we should leave them in a state of confusion with their bereavement. Instead, we need to keep explaining to them what has happened and why they are feeling the way they feel. Explanations need to be basic, real and practical, with a very visual element. Do not rely on words.

Activities to help develop a child's understanding of death

(You may find some of these activities rather strange and morbid, but they really do help to demonstrate what death is to a child.)

- Have a bowl of fruit in the classroom and watch how the fruit shrivels and decays. With the children, try various ways to revive the fruit such as washing the pieces of fruit or placing them in the fridge. The children will see that the fruit is unable to return to the way it was. Compare the bowl of 'dead' fruit to a bowl of fresh 'live' fruit.

- Have a vase of flowers and watch them gradually wilt and die, and then compare these flowers to a vase of living flowers. The children will see that the dead flowers will not come back to life, however much water and sunlight is given to them.

- Have a live fish in a bowl of water for the children to observe and look after. Then buy a small fish from your fishmonger. Let the children look at this dead fish and then place it in a bowl of water. The children will see that even when the dead fish is placed in the bowl of water, it does not come back to life.

- To help students begin to understand what a funeral is, hold a funeral for the fish used in the above activity or for any school pet that dies. Replicate a real funeral as much as possible by having music, hymns/songs, readings and so on. Bury the fish/animal in the school grounds and mark the burial spot. The children can also make a decorative coffin for the fish/animal and a marker for the grave.

- If the class has a small pet such as a stick insect or fish that dies you can use this as a way to help children begin to understand what a cremation is. When the class pet dies you can hold a memorial for the animal and scatter 'its' ashes in the school grounds. Prior to the memorial (and not with the children) burn some leaves (to create ashes) and remove the dead pet from the classroom and dispose of it. Combine the ash of the leaves with some earth (so it's easier for the children to see and to handle) and then use these as the ashes during the memorial service.

- As you do the above activities, take photographs and videos so that you have visual resources and reminders to use with the children in the future.

Activities to help grieving children

- Providing grieving children with physical outlets is an excellent way to give them a temporary release from the grieving process. It allows them to 'get away' from the deep, oppressive feelings of bereavement. However, physical activities also support the grieving process. Whilst engaged in the physical task, they will be able to release emotions physically and this can often lead to emotions being expressed verbally (or through body language, especially for children who are non-verbal). Examples of physical activities include: running outside, climbing (or for children who use a wheelchair, being taken for an exhilarating fast walk or being pushed on a wheelchair swing), throwing balls or beanbags randomly or into/at targets and manipulating/pounding clay or play dough.

- Use photographs of the person who has died. Pass them around at circle time and encourage individuals to share thoughts and emotions about the person if they are willing to do so.

- Use objects related to the individual who died (e.g. an item of their clothing or a favourite toy or book) to help the children talk about the person and share how they are feeling.

- Listen to music that the person who died liked or that relates to them. This may elicit responses and thoughts from the children or may just provide a very happy and reflective session.

- Create a 'stone pile' – every time you share a memory of the person who died add a stone to a decorative bowl. You could write a few words on each stone. This activity could also be done by adding leaves to a decorative tree, flowers into a garden display or whatever other imagery fits with the deceased.

- Choose an activity/routine that the class really identified with the person who has died such as playing a certain game, laying the table for a snack (as this was the child's favourite job to do in class) and so on. As you lead this activity, intentionally talk about the person who has died and how they used to do this task. It can often be much easier to talk about a person who has died when you are actively engaged in doing something that they enjoyed.

- As a class, write a story about the person who has died.

- Emotion stones – have three stones: one jagged, one round and one shiny and smooth. Use these to express different emotions and ways of feeling. The round stone represents normal, everyday feelings; the jagged stone represents difficult emotions; the shiny stone represents special times. Ask the children to choose the stone that they are feeling and if possible to express why they are feeling this way. Even if the child is unable to verbalise how they are feeling, selecting the stone relevant to how they are feeling allows them to communicate their emotions. The opportunity to handle and explore the stone will also be very therapeutic for the child.

- Make friendship bracelets for each other, so the children are reminded of the friends that they still have around them.

- Have extra music therapy sessions. Music therapy is not only educational, enjoyable and relaxing for children, but it also allows them to be expressive in a different way. It allows them to release their thoughts and emotions about the death in a musical manner.

- Each child can make a personal family tree (including friends and family), so that the child can see who they still have around them. This allows them to see who is alive and reminds them that just because one person has died, it doesn't mean that everyone else in their life is going to die straight away too.

- Make a 'life-story' book. Use pictures and photos to make a book telling the story of the child's life up until now. This includes who has died and when and how it happened. The child will be able to read and retell their life story and see how the death of their friend is just a part of their whole life.

- Have a furry toy or a hot water bottle that they can cuddle in times of great sadness or distress.

- Laminate photos of the person who has died so that the children can have them in their bag, classroom tray, locker, at home and so on. They will then be able to look at them whenever they need to.

- Go to a special, happy place – a venue that reminds the child/ children of the person who has died, for example have a trip to the park or a soft play centre.

- As a class, make a memory lantern. This activity is particularly good to do at special times such as birthdays, Christmas, etc. when the person who has died will be especially missed. Have lots of different coloured tissue paper and ask the children to choose a colour and then cut or tear a shape that they can then write or draw a special memory on. Use marker pens, as these work best on the delicate tissue paper. If possible, encourage the children to talk about the memory they are writing or drawing. Then have the children stick their coloured memories to the outside of a glass jar. Continue sticking 'memories' until the jar is covered. Once all available space has been covered, place a tea-light candle or an electrical candle inside the memory lantern.

- Create a memory project with the grieving child – a memory box containing items related to the deceased, a photo album, an item of clothing, their favourite toy, a pillow made from an item of the deceased's clothing and so on. Making this memory box as multisensory as possible allows the child to remember the deceased on many different sensory levels. For sight you could use photos and videos of the person who has died; for hearing an audio CD of the person's voice and a collection of their favourite songs; for taste a few of their favourite things to eat (favourite crisps and biscuits, etc.); for touch a piece of their clothing, a favourite toy or belonging of the person; for smell a bottle of their favourite scent or a smell that they loved or was associated with them, lavender or a special cream and so on.

- Make a 'safe box' – put together a collection of things that help to make the child feel safe: toys, books, games, music, etc. The child will then be able to go to this box when they are feeling vulnerable, and it is hoped that engaging with one of the items in the box will assist in calming them down and/or cheering them up.

- If the child is able to, get them to tell you their top five worries. If they are unable to tell you their worries but you feel that they do have deep concerns, show them 'worry sentences', for example 'I am worried I will die', 'I am worried I have no friends', etc. in symbol/picture/sign format (use their preferred mode of communication). It is hoped that by sharing their worries with someone else and being able to talk about their concerns will lessen the intensity of these worries. Examples of worry sentences are:

- I am worried I will die.

- I am worried I have no friends.

- I am worried Jessie was in pain.

- I am worried that my mum will die.

- I am worried that my dad will die.

- I am worried that my brother will die.

- I am worried that my sister will die.

- I am worried that Nanny will die.

- I am worried that Grandad will die.

- I am worried that you will die.

- I am worried that I will always be sad.

- I am worried about the funeral.

- I am worried that it is wrong to feel happy.

- I am worried that it is wrong to laugh.

- I am worried that Dan died because I was bad.

- I am worried that Dan died because I was horrible to him.

• Create a special bag for the grieving child that has a range of things in it to help them smile, for example a comfort pillow (to be able to hold and cuddle), bubbles (to blow away worries and concerns), a photo album/book, a collection of things/ pictures/photos/jokes that make them smile and comfort cards (see below). This bag needs to be kept close to the child so that they can access it whenever they need to.

• Comfort cards are cards that contain an activity (either in written or pictorial/symbol format) that helps the child to feel better. The child can choose a card (either physically or via eye pointing) and then show it to an adult. Comfort card activities could include:

- ask a friend for a hug
- ask for deep pressure compression, for example being rolled in a blanket or wearing a weighted jacket
- ask for a massage
- take five slow, deep breaths
- put both of my arms around my body and give myself a great big squeeze
- snuggle up with a pillow and a blanket and have a cry
- go to the mirror and pull funny faces to cheer myself up
- blow bubbles and help blow my troubles away
- go for a run around the playground
- be pushed on the swing
- ask for some 'time out'.

By carrying out the activities in this list with a class of children, you will quickly see how different children within the group react and then determine which ones require further individual support.

Providing grieving children with a safe space

Some grieving children may need a bit of time and space alone. You need to be able to provide them with this at school. This space could be a small room adjoining the classroom, the sensory room, the library, a very large cardboard box with cushions and blankets and so on. No matter how small your school is or how limited the space, there are always ways of creating a 'safe space' for the child to have some quiet time. If a child is able to ask to spend some time in this safe space, this shows they are developing good self-regulatory skills.

Remember: although children may request time alone, they always need to be monitored. This can, however, easily be done without disturbing their need for solitude.

Children who are non-verbal should also have the means to ask for time in this safe space and this can be done by them pressing a switch (that says 'quiet time please' or however you choose to describe this space), by signing, eye pointing to a symbol, reaching for the object of reference and so on.

How to talk to grieving children

- Use clear language.

- Accept that there will be questions and be prepared to answer any and all questions to the best of your ability.

- Always be open, honest and available. The death of a child's family member or someone in your school community is no time to be a slave to the timetable. How can a child learn if they are in a state of emotional distress?

- Words are important. Always use the appropriate words and not euphemisms, for example use the words 'dead' and 'death' not 'just sleeping' and so on.

- Be patient. Be prepared to explain things over and over again, so the child can process and accept the death. You may have to answer the same questions again and again, but by doing so you are providing the pupil with comfort and reassurance.

- When you have given the child information, such as about the death and what will be happening next, regularly check that they have understood what you have told them, but do not repeatedly ask them 'Do you understand?' Instead, check their understanding through conversational routes, for example if you have told them that the funeral for the deceased person is on Thursday, later on ask them if they remember what is happening on Thursday.

Specific things to say when talking to children about loss

- Your feelings are normal.

- You aren't the only person feeling this way.

- I know that you feel upset/angry/sad/lonely/scared, etc.

- Acknowledge comments made by the child by saying things such as 'Yes', 'Right' and 'I understand.'

Do not do/say the following when talking to children about loss

- Interrupt the child when they are talking about their feelings or experiences.

- Repeatedly ask them 'Do you understand?'

- Bombard them with questions.

- Make statements such as:

  - 'I know how you feel.'

  - 'Don't cry.'

  - 'Don't be angry.'

  - 'You'll get over it in time.'

Things to remember when working with children who have experienced a bereavement

- Know the basic facts of how the person died so that you are able to answer the child's questions and help embed their understanding of the death.

- Answer questions clearly and accurately.

- Make sure the child is aware of the funeral, memorial service, etc. and is involved as much as they would like to be (this will be discussed further in Chapter 13).

- Get the child involved in a whole-school 'goodbye ritual' (this will be discussed in Chapter 22) to help them say goodbye and/ or a personal goodbye, such as releasing a balloon, blowing bubbles, planting a tree and so on.

- Make time for physical outlets of expression.

- Provide creative outlets for expression.

- Maintain routines and structures as far as possible, but allow for flexibility – you need to follow the needs of the bereaved child.

After a loss, children need to regain a sense of safety and stability – how is this achieved?

- All of the child's basic needs must be met first (food, drink, warmth, safety and security).
- Re-establish the child's routines.
- Parents/carers/school staff need to have support systems in place for themselves and the child.
- Teach/support emotional regulation skills, for example asking for 'time out', using relaxation and breathing techniques (more on this in Chapter 20).
- Provide lots of 'the ordinary' (even though you might think they need lots of 'special time').

Building resilience in bereaved children

A child's resilience has a great deal to do with their self-esteem: what they know, what they can do well, what they have and what they can rely on. For children who are grieving, building resilience is especially important.

We cannot take away the child's sadness, but we can help them through the loss by supporting the child to feel better about themselves by teaching them skills to manage their emotions, worries and uncertainties that the death will have given them. This all contributes to developing the child's resilience.

Ways to help build resilience

- Make sure the child knows they are lovable and that they are loved.
- Reassure them about who is still there for them (who cares for them, who their friends are and so on).
- Make sure they know that not everyone is suddenly going to die.
- Keep routines as normal as possible.
- Keep expectations as normal as possible.

- Encourage them to express their feelings, thoughts and emotions.

- Make sure they know that it's OK for everything *not* to be overshadowed by the loss. It's right and proper for them still to have fun, laugh and be children.

- Ask them what they think about certain things and truly listen to their answers.

- Give them choices when it is possible to do so.

- Make them a part of the decision making (again, when it is appropriate and possible to do so).

- Explain to them that whilst they are coping with their grief, they may feel and behave differently at times.

- Acknowledge that they have experienced difficult times.

- Give them praise and show that you believe in them.

Feelings of loss and grief don't disappear at the end of a school year. These are lifelong emotions that can be triggered by any number of experiences or memories and thus it is imperative that information regarding a child's bereavement is passed on to the next teacher and staff group.

And don't forget that each and every experience of death will be different, we are all individuals and every situation is unique. Therefore, there is no one solution for dealing with grief.

CHAPTER 12

Advice for Supporting Individuals with Autistic Spectrum Disorders (ASD)

Children with ASD need their grief acknowledged and supported just as any other child does. Just because a child with ASD may not respond to a death in a manner that is similar to other children, this does not mean that they are not grieving.

Following a bereavement, individuals with ASD may be more impulsive in their behaviour and reactions, and they can struggle to understand what other people are feeling and thinking. This 'mind blindness' means that children with ASD may not see how a death is impacting on those around them. This may result in them appearing unaffected by the death and uncaring of others and seemingly acting inappropriately. They will also struggle to see how others can help them with their own grief.

Language

The correct use of language concerning death and bereavement is important with all children, but it is vitally important for children with ASD. They will take everything you say literally. You must ensure that you do not use any type of euphemisms. Instead, give them accurate information at a level appropriative to their cognitive functioning, carefully balancing how much information you give them at any one time. Take the lead from the child and be prepared to reiterate details and scaffold their understanding and acceptance of the information.

A bereavement can cause an increase in the child's known behaviours and some new behaviours can appear. It can also trigger and increase their obsessions, fears and phobias and heighten their resistance to change.

If the child has language, it is still highly probable that they will struggle to find the words to express how they are truly feeling. This is why providing children with goodbye rituals and ways to express themselves that don't merely rely on words is so very important. (See Chapter 22 for further information on ways you can encourage children to express their grief.)

> The reaction of a child with ASD to a death and the language they use may appear to be indifferent, inappropriate or even callous.

This should in no way be misunderstood or criticised. It demonstrates how the child currently understands the death (possibly in a very clinical manner) and the child's need for further education and support with emotional understanding and processing.

It is important to provide children with ASD with information in non-verbal ways; do not rely on spoken words. Use symbols, social stories and comic-style cartoons. Comic-strip type conversations/social stories can be very useful, as the graphics can clearly represent the emotions being felt by those who are grieving.

Children with ASD generally connect with far fewer individuals than typically developing children, so the loss of someone who they were close to is often felt as an even greater catastrophic event. Following the loss, they may also be more reluctant to develop other relationships, fearing that if they get close to someone they too may die.

Sensory issues

Often individuals with ASD have great sensory issues, for example having a heightened awareness of sounds, smells, light and textures. Being in a grieving environment can often result in many new and different sensory experiences. There may be lots of flowers around giving off a strong scent, changes in lighting and sounds to reflect the mood of the situation, visits to different buildings with different sensory situations, such as a church with hard pews or a graveyard with the strong smell of newly cut grass. All of these new situations have the potential to trigger anxieties in a person with ASD, and as far as possible we need to be aware of difficult things that they encounter and prepare them accordingly.

The sensory impact of clothing can also be significant, and if children with ASD are given new and more formal clothing to wear for a funeral or memorial service, this may be immensely stressful for them. The harder textures of the new clothes and confinement of a suit, dress, etc. can all lead to a greater level of anxiety.

Sharing the news

Be prepared that sometimes the person sharing the news of the death can be the person who a child directs their anger towards.

Staff need to provide genuine comfort and support for children with ASD who are grieving. We should not rush them through their grief and we must never tell them to get over it. Their feelings should be respected and the difficult process that they will be going through should be acknowledged. This isn't just for a matter of weeks or months; it is for life.

No one knows when a loss is going to affect someone. Years after a death, something such as a song or a place can quickly trigger memories of a deceased loved one. If the initial grieving process wasn't handled correctly, this new grief will be made even more difficult. However, if the child has been supported well initially, these triggered thoughts and memories can be happy reflective times rather than ones plunging them into full-on grief.

Tough questions

Some children with ASD will want a lot of detail about the death and they will have a great number of questions for you. You may not be prepared for some of these questions or may be shocked by them, for example 'How long will it take for the body to turn into a skeleton?' or 'Did they start to smell as soon as they died?' The child isn't asking these types of questions because they are being morbid or macabre; knowing these details will help them to understand and in turn to cope with the death.

For a parent or someone who was very close to the person who has died, these questions may be too difficult to handle. Instead, find a person who is comfortable to answer these hard questions and who the child knows well. You can then 'teach' the child to go to this adult with these sorts of questions.

Difficulties that a child with ASD may experience

- Children with ASD can often struggle to see things from another person's perspective and, therefore, may not see or understand that others are grieving, too. Also, they may not comprehend that there are people who can help support them with their grief.

- It's hard for them to conceptualise death and its rituals as these things are too abstract and beyond their norm. They are not tangible things that they can grasp.

- Information processing is difficult for them as they are unable to extrapolate things, such as someone having died meaning that they won't be able to take them swimming on Saturday (something that they have always done).

- Language and communication difficulties mean that understanding the abstract concepts surrounding death is very complicated. Remember, do not talk in euphemisms and be concrete with your explanations and terminology.

- Difficulties with imagination and time perception mean it is hard for them to see how the death will affect them in the future.

- The preoccupations/obsessions of a child with ASD may become more extreme due to their anxiety following the death.

If it is known that the death is imminent, it would be beneficial (if possible) to prepare the child for the death. (You can help to do this with the live/dead activities in Chapter 11.)

Things to remember when talking about a death with someone who has autism ASD (and good practice for all children with SEND)

- Try to speak at a similar speed and level as the child.
- Always sit alongside the child and at their eye level.
- Tell them that they will be listened to and continue to remind them of this.

- Make sure the child knows that they can ask questions.

- Answer their questions immediately.

- Don't be afraid to say 'I don't know' or 'I'll try to find out' to any questions that you don't know the answer to.

- Always accept their feelings.

- Make sure you allow enough time/silence to enable the child to be able to process what they are being told and also ensure they can express their thoughts and feelings.

- Echo back to the child what they have said to you but in a slightly different way. This reinforces that you have listened to them and also helps them embed their processing of the loss.

Note: All other advice and activities contained in this book also apply to children with ASD.

It is hoped that care, time and support will be the best ingredients for helping a child with ASD through the loss, but there are certain things you should look out for. If you see the child exhibiting any of the behaviours listed below, you need to discuss with their parents the need for a referral to a doctor, counsellor, psychiatrist or educational psychologist.

- They continuously deny that the person has died, even after detailed support and teaching about the death.

- They act as if nothing has happened (not just in the short term but for a significant period of time) when the deceased person was very close to them.

- They become withdrawn (or are more so than normal).

- They threaten or talk about suicide.

Endeavour to keep routines as 'normal' and consistent as possible.

CHAPTER 13

Talking about Funerals, Cremations and Burials

Often, people's immediate thought regarding funerals and other rituals of death is that young children and children with SEND should not attend such occasions.

Children with SEND should not be automatically left out of attending funerals or memorial services. Instead, think through the needs of the child and the way in which the service is taking place.

> Children who have experienced the death of a significant person need to be involved in some sort of 'goodbye' service. Attending such an event helps them to come to terms with the death and begin to think about and understand a world without this person.

The family needs to think carefully about whether the funeral/ memorial service is being held in a manner that makes it accessible and appropriate for the individual to attend. If it is, 'ask' the child (in a mode of communication that is appropriate to them) if they'd like to go.

If it isn't appropriate for the child to attend the funeral, it is crucial to have some type of ceremony that they can attend so they have their opportunity to say 'goodbye'. If this doesn't take place with the family, it makes having a special assembly/memorial service at school even more pertinent. (There is more information on holding a special assembly/memorial service in Chapter 22.)

Funerals, burials and cremations

The child will inevitability hear the funeral, burial or cremation being discussed, either at home or at school, therefore it is important that these concepts are explained to them in terms that they understand. The unknown nature of these events will be far more distressing than being given a basic explanation of what they are. The notes and activities below explain how to do this.

Involving the child

If someone close to the child has died, it is very beneficial for the family to involve the child in the planning of the funeral as far as is practically possible. If this doesn't happen then as a school you should endeavour to involve them in the planning and delivery of the school's assembly/memorial, to the level that they are comfortable with.

Taking a child to a funeral

If you took a typically developing baby, toddler or young child to a funeral they would not understand the service at the time, but as they got older they would know (either from their own memories or being told) that they were with their family at a very important event. This will help them to feel close to their family and, like the rest of the family and friends, to have a 'relationship' with the deceased.

Deciding whether to take a child with SEND to a funeral is a very difficult decision to make and is obviously one to be made by the parents. However, as a teacher, you may be asked for your opinion. Something to consider is whether the child is likely to develop an understanding of death in the coming years. If it is thought that they might and the service is being conducted in a manner that will not unduly distress them, then (like a typically developing toddler) it may be appropriate to take them to the service.

For some children (if they were very close to the deceased), visiting the dead body *may* be appropriate, but this is something that needs *very careful* consideration by the parents and detailed preparation for the child in advance of doing so. For some children (possibly children with ASD), seeing the body – watching to see that there is no breathing, that the skin has changed, the body is cold and so on – can help them see that the body is no longer working and the person has died. This, in turn, can greatly support their overall understanding of the death. It is very rare that seeing the dead person's body is appropriate for a child, but in some circumstances it will be worth considering.

How to explain what a funeral is

'When someone dies, we have a special service so that everyone can get together to remember them. We think about the person who has died, remembering things that they did in their life and how much we love them. The funeral is also a way of us saying a special goodbye to that person.'

How to explain what happens at a funeral
'[Name]'s body will be in a special box called a coffin. This special box has a lid on it, so we will not be able to see [name]'s body. Remember [name] is dead, s/he is no longer alive, her/his body doesn't work and so s/he doesn't need it anymore.

We will go to the church/crematorium/mosque/synagogue/ temple, etc. and the brown wooden box [describe it as accurately as possible to prepare the child fully – showing them a picture/ photo of what the coffin will look like is a good idea] the coffin will be brought to the front of the church/crematorium/mosque/ synagogue/temple, etc. There will be lots of people at the funeral, people who knew [name]. Some people will stand up and say things about [name]. We will listen to some lovely music and we will sing songs/hymns. People at the funeral will be very sad that [name] is no longer alive and some may cry – you may feel like crying. If people do or don't cry and how much they cry doesn't matter.

At the end of the funeral, [name]'s body will be taken away to be buried in the churchyard/cemetery, but we will all be going to [place] to have some food and a drink with all of the family and friends of [name].'

Or: 'At the end of the funeral [name]'s body will be taken away to be cremated. Someone else does this – we will all be going to [place] to have some food and drink with all of the family and friends of [name].'

How to explain a burial
'After the funeral service, the coffin will be taken to the church graveyard/cemetery. At the graveyard/cemetery, a big hole will have been dug in the ground – this is called a grave. [Name]'s coffin will be slowly lowered into the grave and then it will be covered up with earth. The imam/priest/rabbi/vicar, etc. will say a few words before we all leave.

Later on, when the family are ready, a special marker called a headstone will be put on [name]'s grave. This will have her/his name on it so everybody knows that s/he is buried there.

Eventually grass will grow over the grave. We will be able to visit the grave sometimes so that we can remember [name] and we might bring flowers to put on the grave, maybe [flower] as [name] really liked [flower].'

How to explain a cremation

Deciding whether to explain the cremation will need a lot of consideration and will depend greatly on the age and understanding of the child. It may be inappropriate to use words such as burnt or burning with some children, as this can cause great distress. Children are taught about the dangers of fire, the need to keep away from it, so they may not understand why someone they love is being put in such a dangerous situation.

Here is a possible way of explaining a cremation:

'After the funeral [name]'s body will go to the crematorium to be turned into soft powdery ashes. The ashes are then put into a special pot called an urn. The urn will be given to the family. Some people decide to bury the ashes in the ground and some decide to scatter the ashes somewhere that was special to the person who has died. The family don't have to decide this straight away, they can think about it later on.'

Visiting the burial place

For some children, visiting the burial place or the spot where the ashes were scattered can be very comforting and a good way to help with the grieving process. Other children, because of the television programmes and films they may have seen, will believe that graveyards are spooky, scary places. Reassure these children that this is just 'make-believe' and real cemeteries are not like this. It's probably unwise to take children to cemeteries if they believe them to be spooky places. Also, children who are still struggling to comprehend what being dead means may not benefit from visiting the grave. Developing their understanding of death first would be advisable (such as through the activities shown in Chapter 11).

CHAPTER 14

All Forms of Grief and Loss

Although the main focus of this book has been about dealing with grief that is related to death, other forms of grief and loss have been mentioned too, as children need to be supported through all losses, not just those related to a death.

This chapter takes a look at all of the different forms of grief and loss that a child may experience.

This includes grief related to:

- parents/close family members divorcing or separating
- moving house and away from those they are closest to
- people close to them moving away
- changing school
- a pet dying
- the loss of a favourite toy or belonging
- the death of a fictional character or entity and death of someone whom they did not really know
- losing their home and/or belongings due to natural disasters, such as fire or flooding.

Parents/close family members divorcing or separating

A child's parents (or a couple whom they are very close to) telling them that they are separating or getting a divorce takes a great deal of explanation and processing for any child, but this can be especially difficult for a child with SEND.

First, you need to explain to the child what divorce/separation actually is, as this isn't necessarily a term/concept that they will be familiar with. Then you must talk about what the divorce/separation means for the child – the practical changes it will bring about. Next you have to ensure that the child understands that they aren't responsible for the couple breaking up. Finally (and this is the most complex part), you must support the child through the emotional process of coming to terms with the break-up.

All of these stages need a great deal of time, care and sensitivity, and you must ensure that you employ the most appropriate modes of communication and support for the child.

An example of how to tell a child that their parents/close family members are separating is below. Use signs, symbols, objects of reference and the like (whatever the child's preferred mode of communication is) to express this information.

'Mummy and Daddy [or whoever it is] love you very much and always will. Mummy and Daddy aren't happy with each other anymore and they need to live in separate houses. They have some adult problems that they cannot fix, but none of their problems are to do with you. Mummy and Daddy will always love you and will always take care of you. Daddy is going to live in a new house, not far away and you will stay living in the house with Mummy and your brother [or whoever the other family members are]. You will still see Daddy, you will go and see him at his new house and you will go out together.'

Moving house and away from those that they are closest to

Moving house means leaving behind people, places and things that you love. Children will have no experience of moving somewhere new and there being the opportunity to find more people, places and things that they love. The child may just see all that they are losing and be very anxious about the plethora of changes being heaped upon them. Communicate with the child the reason for the move, for example Mummy's new job or moving to live closer to Grandma, and then show them physically (such as the new things that they can do, the people they will see and so on) and with explanations (supported by signs, symbols, objects of reference, etc.) all that is good about their new area and home.

People close to the child moving away

When someone close to the child moves away, the child may struggle to see how they will cope without them and may believe that they will never see them again. They will need to be shown that moving away doesn't mean that the person is gone forever. Teach the child how they can still keep in touch with their friend/family member via the telephone, Skype, text messaging, social media, letters, cards and visits. Although this doesn't lessen the loss, the child may also need reminding that they still have other friends close by and that there will be opportunities to make new friends. This will take time; first they need to adjust to the changes that the move brings to their life and, as with all losses, they need to acclimatise to a new 'normal'.

Changing school

Moving school means a great number of practical changes, as well as emotional challenges. There will be a new journey to school, a new uniform, a new building, new teachers, a new classroom and new friends. All children seek stability and crave routines and for children with SEND this need for consistency is increased. When a child moves school, a great deal of time is required to prepare them for the move and gradually introduce them to the new environment. They may well mourn for the school they have left, their friends and teachers, etc. and you will need to support them through this difficult transition with time, understanding and care. Communicate with the child the reason for the move, for example moving house or the old school closing, and then show them (physically and with explanations) all that is good about their new school.

As part of the transition process from one school to another, it is good for parents/carers/families to take their child for a few visits to the new school so that they can start to meet the staff and other children. If the school doesn't provide 'a new school' booklet with photos of the new classroom, staff, other pupils, etc., ask for one to be made so the family can have lots of time to look at it with the child at home and so it can be used in the current school to help support the child with the move.

It is beneficial for parents to buy the new school uniform in advance of the child starting at the new school so that the child can look at it and start to get used to the colours, texture and fit. Also, practising the journey to the new school will help to familiarise the child with the route and alleviate some of their fears.

A pet dying

Pets are members of our families. When a pet dies, whether it is a hamster, dog, stick insect or horse, the impact of the death can be great for the child. Children are often very close to the animals in their lives – they are someone that they can talk to without any judgements being made, they provide unconditional love and they are a source of calming properties and great comfort. When a child's pet dies you need to handle this bereavement as you would any other bereavement.

Loss of a favourite toy or belonging

We all put a great deal of significance into different objects. Children are no exception; the cheapest, tattiest toy can hold deep emotional attachment for a child. Treat any loss that the child experiences as a genuine loss, however hard it is for you to understand. The disappearance of that special stone they collected on a beach ten years ago may be hard for you to understand. You may think, 'But it's just a stone, we can pick another one up anywhere.' But the child remembers that they collected the stone with Grandad, on the day that he showed them how to fly a kite. Grandad has since died and that stone is a very strong connection for them to him.

Remember, children can experience grief over things that may seem very small and insignificant for an adult. The loss of a possession that they have had since being a toddler can be catastrophic for them. We must not underestimate or devalue these losses.

Think about how you would feel if you lost your mobile phone – many adults would probably be totally distraught. In the grand scheme of things, losing a mobile phone is fairly inconsequential but at the time it can feel as if we have lost a part of our life – how will we manage without it? This is the same for children when they lose something special to them, whatever it is.

Death of a fictional character or entity and death of someone whom they did not really know

When a character on a television show or in a book, etc. dies, children can mourn this loss as significantly as the death of a close relative. The child will have got to know this character/person over a long period of time and they will feel that they know them extremely well. The 'death' of this person may impact them in just the same way as a real death, and we must not dismiss the significance of the death to them.

The same sense of grief and loss will apply to a child (who identified strongly with a particular band) when the band breaks up.

Finally, there will be many actors and celebrities that our children identify with and, although they will not have met these people, they will feel that they know them due to the amount of information they know about them from social media, television, magazines, etc. Therefore, this death will also be significant to the child and they will need support to come to terms with it.

Losing their home and/or belongings due to natural disasters, such as fire or flooding

A natural disaster, such as a fire or flood, affecting the home will be devastating for anyone (unless they are very skilled at not placing strong attachments to their home and its contents) – child or adult.

Such natural disasters mean that precious belongings are lost, our environment is changed (at the very least temporarily) and as a result our routines have to alter. All of these things result in increased anxiety for children, especially those with SEND.

This is a loss that you cannot prepare or plan for – it just happens – and following such a disaster you have to help guide the child through the situation by providing as many 'normal' routines and activities as possible. Being able to go to school and see their friends will help a lot, and, if possible, being able to salvage a couple of significant items from the house for the child to have with them will provide them with a connection to their 'normal' life.

Finally, keeping the child informed of what is happening (to the level that they will be able to comprehend), answering their questions and reassuring them that they are safe are all very important.

Individuals experiencing any of these forms of grief tend to encounter the same areas of grief processing as with a death:

1. shock/denial

2. anger

3. depression

4. bargaining

5. acceptance.

But remember, grief does not come in easy, linear steps; we tend to move backwards and forwards and in and out of the various stages until we finally reach a point of acceptance.

You need to help children work through the forms of grief and loss discussed in this chapter as you would a bereavement (as explained in Chapters 8 to 11) and, even once acceptance is achieved, children (like adults) may still have events or occurrences that trigger the emotions of a loss, resulting in them needing support to come to terms with it all over again.

CHAPTER 15

Traumatic Losses

All deaths and losses can be very sad and difficult to come to terms with. This chapter focuses on traumatic deaths and losses. These could be deaths that have occurred in very difficult circumstances, such as suicide and murder, and experiencing tragic situations that result in a person grieving for a part of their life that they have lost, such as losses resulting from rape or sexual assault.

Traumatic deaths include:

- suicide
- murder
- stillbirth
- miscarriage
- death in military action – the armed forces
- sudden death.

Traumatic losses include:

- rape
- sexual assault
- assault
- burglary.

The level to which these traumatic deaths and losses are explained to the child has to be dependent on their cognitive understanding. To begin with, you may only give a very small amount of information, but be prepared to answer any and all of the child's questions, however hard and upsetting this is (if the questions are too hard for you to answer then it's advisable to have another person available to answer them). The unknown is always more frightening than being informed; the child needs to have their questions answered and know that there is someone there to support them through this difficult time. As the child gets older and gradually understands a little more of what has happened, they will probably have more questions – they will seek more details about what happened and why.

Children who experience the very traumatic deaths and losses listed above can be well supported by members of staff whom they are close to at school – caring individuals who are there for the child to talk to and are always available to provide reassurance. However, dealing with the complex emotional scars of such traumatic losses and deaths will probably result in the child needing professional counselling and/or psychological support.

As members of the school community, you will be with the child on a daily basis, enabling you to provide a sense of normality and to give on-going care and security to the child. This is an immensely important part of the child's overall recovery. Provide this support in the same way you would for other grief, but do not confuse this support with external professional treatment. Psychiatric support for such complex cases must be carried out by trained professionals.

These two levels of support and guidance (psychiatric and in-school) go hand in hand, and both are required for the child to be able to move on successfully with their life.

CHAPTER 16

When to Refer Children to Other Professionals

As previously mentioned, you do not need to be a trained counsellor or psychiatrist to help the bereaved children with whom you work. As the class teacher, teaching assistant, etc. of a grieving child you will know that child incredibly well and will generally be able to help and support them with their grief, but we must be open to seeing when the child requires further professional support and be prepared for this. A member of school staff can assist a great deal, but some children may require the assistance of a doctor, counsellor, psychologist or psychiatrist. If they do, this in no way means that you have failed them. The support you have given them and the work that you have done will have been beneficial, but they now need a little extra guidance.

When should you refer a child to another professional? Look out for the following behaviours.

- They refuse to acknowledge that the person has died – even after detailed support and teaching about the death (and even though they were very close to the person who has died).

- They act as if nothing has changed (not just in the short term, but for a significant period of time) even though they were very close to the deceased person.

- They start to suffer with panic attacks.

- They are harming themselves or others.

- They become withdrawn (or are more so than normal). This is where it is important to know the individual well, so you can recognise differences from their 'norm'.

- They talk about suicide or threaten to commit suicide.

- They become involved in extreme anti-social behaviour.
- They start to use drugs or alcohol.

If you become aware of the child or young person doing any of these things, you need to talk to their parents immediately and together refer the grieving child to other professionals, such as a doctor, counsellor, psychologist or psychiatrist.

Staff

CHAPTER 17

How to Support Staff

When working in SEND environments, bereavements are sadly a part of our professional lives because of the medical challenges faced by some of our children. Being as prepared and informed as possible may not lessen the grief associated with a pupil dying, but it does help to manage it more effectively.

Following the death of a pupil, staff may experience the following

- Shock
- Operating on autopilot
- Emotional detachment
- Fear
- Anxiety
- Uncertainty
- Denial
- Loneliness
- Blame
- Numbness
- Depression
- Anger
- Sadness
- Irritability
- Sense of guilt (could they have done more for the child while they were alive?)
- Relief (e.g. because the child had been in pain for a long time)
- Concern about doing and saying the right thing

Staff may also experience the following possible physical effects

- Tearfulness

- Tiredness

- Feeling on edge

- Lack of concentration

- Insomnia

- Dreams/nightmares

- Headaches

- Stomach aches

- Upset stomach

A school's headteacher and her/his leadership team have a duty of care to their staff as well as the pupils. Following the death of a pupil, the 'Crisis Team' (see Chapters 28 and 29 for further information on the Crisis Team) should meet to discuss whether there are any staff that are particularly vulnerable to the news and who will require extra support. A 'Crisis Team' is made up of members of the school staff. Each member has a role assigned to them to carry out following a death or similar crisis. The team should meet with all staff to discuss the ways they may be affected by the bereavement (see the lists at the start of this chapter) and to share tips to help staff manage their feelings and work through the grieving process. This should include details of how and when support can be provided to them and by whom.

Ways staff can help manage their feelings

- Talk to others.

- Listen to others.

- Use colleagues as sounding boards to talk through issues and concerns, etc.

- Make sure you have someone you can talk to.

- Give yourself time – don't rush any stage of the grieving process. Every stage ultimately helps you deal with the loss.

- Look after yourself and the physical aspects of grief (e.g. extreme tiredness – make sure you have plenty of rest).

- Look after yourself – this isn't an indulgence or extravagance; it is fundamental. If you don't look after yourself, your health will suffer and you will not be able to support and take care of the pupils to the best of your ability. Ignoring these signs may result in you being off work due to ill health, meaning you will be completely unable to support the grieving child.

- Have plenty of physical activity – take the dog for a walk, have a stroll in the park, etc. Getting out and about and moving around allows your mind to 'refresh' and think about other things.

- Take part in activities and hobbies that you enjoy; this will occupy you and allow you to think about different things.

- Try to eat and drink even if you don't feel like it.

- Keep an eye on changes in your eating and drinking (e.g. an increased consumption of alcoholic drinks).

- Don't mask feelings with alcohol or through other extremes (e.g. obsessive exercising, drugs).

- Keep your routines as normal as possible.

- Ensure that you make time each day for you, even if it's just a quiet five minutes.

- Actively do things to help you relax.

- Be aware of the support that's available at your workplace so that you know what to do and who to see if you need help.

- Remember that there are many reactions to grief. Grief may affect you a lot or not at all (or not immediately) and that grief can sometimes catch you unawares.

- Find your own way to say goodbye to the person who has died.

- Develop your memories of the person who has died – remember the good times.

- Just take one day at a time.

The different aspects of mourning

- Coming to terms with the death and accepting that it has happened.
- Living through the physical and emotional effects of the loss.
- Acclimatising to a world where the person is no more.
- Finding ways to remember the person.

If staff have training that explains these emotions and reactions to the death, they will be more likely to recognise them in themselves and in their colleagues. This will promote a more positive and supportive grieving community.

As teachers and teaching staff, we have to keep a close eye on how our pupils are coping with a loss. Senior leaders of a school must do the same for their staff. By doing this, they not only take good care of their colleagues, but in turn they also ensure that the pupils are being well supported with their grief, because they will be surrounded by staff who are 'positive role models of grief'.

How staff can help other staff members

- Acknowledge their loss.
- Ask if they would like to talk (if you do this, make sure you have the time to do so).
- Be with them. They may not want to talk but instead may require the closeness and support of someone being there for them.
- Allow them to cry and be sad. Don't stifle their emotions.
- Never minimise their emotions and feelings.
- Recognise that everyone grieves in their own individual way.
- Be honest – talk about the facts, what is known and unknown about the death and if there are things that cannot be discussed, explain why this is the case.
- Maintain routines as much as possible.

- Don't compare losses and levels of grief (this can be very insensitive, it isn't a competition to see who is affected the most by the death; everyone will be affected in their own way).

When a member of staff looks for extra support, think about addressing the following things

- Make sure the member of staff understands the facts regarding the death and that they have the opportunity to ask questions.

- Provide the opportunity for the member of staff to talk about their professional connection and relationship to the child who has died and how this is affecting their reaction to the death.

- Give staff the space to normalise their reaction to the event (e.g. understand why they feel the way that they do).

- Be supportive. Make sure that the member of staff understands that this isn't a one-off chance to talk, but rather, that you are there for them whenever they need you.

- Look for any signs that the person requires further professional support.

Signs that members of staff may require further support

- They are finding it hard to cope.
- Their work, home or social life is suffering.
- They are having repeated thoughts about death or dying.
- They are losing or gaining a significant amount of weight.
- They are talking to other people, but they feel as if their friends/colleagues are tired of listening or are unable to help.

If you see signs like these in a colleague, you need to meet with them and discuss the possible need for further professional support, either through their doctor, school/local authority counselling service or a private referral.

Max Strom said in his book, *A Life Worth Breathing*: 'The body, emotions and mind are not separate. If we stuff our emotions down into our body, the emotions can, in their way, fester and then literally become illness' (Strom, 2010, p.109).

And finally, remember…

- We all grieve differently.

- To better support others with their grief, we must first look at our own experiences of death and loss and consider how we managed the experience and associated emotions.

- Grief does not come in tidy stages; it can be confusing and chaotic.

- Sadly, sometimes it does get worse before it gets better.

- You may find comfort in unexpected things or places – be open to this.

- It's OK to cry sometimes and it's OK *not* to cry sometimes.

- Grief triggers are everywhere – you will see and hear things that remind you of the person all over the place and, at times, this may lead to rapid expression of emotion.

- Birthdays, anniversaries and big life events related to the deceased person will possibly be difficult forever.

- Having counselling or any form of therapy in no way makes you weak or crazy.

CHAPTER 18

Staff Emotions and the School Day

A school community and its leadership team have a duty of care to pupils and staff. As already noted, staff will undoubtedly be affected by the death of a pupil or someone within (or close to) the school community. This book has looked at the many ways to help and support staff (see Chapters 5 and 17).

There will, however, be days when some staff are more affected than others, for example in the first few days after the death or when a significant date (the deceased person's birthday) or perhaps something in their own life triggers intense emotions.

We want our children to have healthy grief role models. Therefore, seeing adults who are sad or shed a few tears (e.g. when the class sings the deceased child's favourite song) is all very appropriate.

However, a member of staff who is clearly very distressed is not best placed in the classroom. This is a time when they need care and support outside the classroom, because they will be unable to carry out their job safely and to the standard that the pupils deserve. We cannot forget that the school has to carry on and the children continue to deserve an excellent education and level of care. Also, the children will become very concerned and possibly frightened if they see a member of staff completely distraught. Therefore, following a pupil bereavement the school should have extra/flexible staffing arrangements in place so that members of staff who are overly affected during the school day know that if they need to take some time out of the classroom to compose themselves, this is perfectly acceptable. A member of staff who is struggling more than this (e.g. they need more than a few minutes out of class to compose themselves) probably needs to see their doctor or a counsellor for some extra support. A member of the leadership team should talk to them about such a referral.

In my experience, staff who were very close to a child who has died say that being in class with the other pupils is the best way for them to cope and it helps them come to terms with the loss. The camaraderie of the class and the joy that other pupils bring (by carrying out the simplest, everyday things) give them a sense of normality and provides them with the purpose to carry on.

When we step into a classroom at the beginning of any school day, there is a sense of stepping into a 'performance': putting on your 'show face' and getting on with the job in hand. This in no way diminishes our loss. Rather, this routine helps us to carry on with daily life.

CHAPTER 19

Staff Dos and Don'ts

The following staff dos and don'ts are in relation to what to do and say with grieving pupils; however, they also apply to grieving colleagues.

Staff dos

Do...

- Listen, listen and listen again.

- Sit beside children at their eye level when talking to them about the death.

- Speak at a speed similar to that which they speak/understand.

- Give the child time to talk and be with you – have regular sessions (that are not too long) to talk about their grief, rather than one long session.

- Always be available to listen and comfort (this can't just be at scheduled times – you have to take the lead from the child's emotions and state of mind).

- Make sure the child knows they will always be listened to.

- Ensure the child understands that they are allowed to ask questions and then answer the questions immediately.

- Be honest and say 'I don't know' or 'I'll try to find out for you' if you don't have an answer to a child's question.

- Share the facts about the death with them.

- Keep all explanations simple and concise.

- Always accept a child's feelings. Never dismiss or undervalue them.

- Allow the child to cry and allow them to express themselves however they need to (as long as this doesn't put themselves or others in danger).

- Look for behavioural changes in the child; this will give you clues as to how they are coping.

- Be knowledgeable about your students. You need to know about previous bereavements, losses and any mental health issues that they have experienced.

- Be informed of the child's (and their family's) beliefs and cultural background, specifically how this relates to death. These can impact greatly on how the child will cope and come to terms with death, as well as how you should support them.

- Support the child within their usual schedules, routines and rituals, using their typical reward structures.

- Remind the child that the death is not their fault.

- Ensure children are recognised as mourners and grievers.

- Treat each child and their grief as individual and unique.

- Give the child different options and choices about being involved in the rituals of death (sending condolence cards, attending memorials and so on) wherever possible.

- Promote consistency and stick to routines as far as possible.

- Talk about and remember the person who has died.

- Make a safe environment for the child to grieve in.

- Be a model of 'healthy grief'.

- Give reassurance and affection.

- Be patient.

- Prepare for *all* of the different emotions that the child might display.

- Have a wide variety of resources and activities to hand through which the children can explore their grief.

- Remember that playing is a part of grieving for a child.

- Make sure the child knows that they are not alone in having to come to terms with the death.

- Take breaks from grieving. The teacher/member of staff may have to structure this into the school day if the child is locked into grief, for example times when there is an activity that will really motivate the child to be engaged and perhaps not be consumed with grief.

- Have good parent–school/teacher communication so that everyone knows how the child is doing in different situations.
- Have signposting to other support agencies/professionals in place and be ready to share with families and staff, as required.
- Have activities and resources (for explaining the death and dealing with the death) prepared and ready to use.
- Always give clear direct information.
- Remember and mark special days.
- Look after your own grief.
- Remember to take care of yourself.

Staff don'ts

Don't…

- Think that the child does not feel the loss.
- Assume that a child with a cognitive and/or physical impairment will not understand the loss and therefore will not need support.
- Ignore their emotions, thoughts and opinions on the loss.
- Tell the child not to be sad – they are unable to control their emotions and nor should they have to.
- Force children to talk.
- Be afraid of moments of silence when talking with children; these periods of quiet give the child time to reflect and digest information.
- Hide your own sadness.
- Lie or tell a half-truth.
- Make sudden or unexpected changes to their schedule/routine.
- Feel as if you have to have all of the answers all of the time.
- Be surprised or question a child's true grief when they are able to put their grief to one side and get on with life for a little while.

- Think that you are unable to support them. The school staff who work with these children every day are the very best placed people to support them because they know them so well.

- Talk in euphemisms or give them white lies. This only causes problems that need to be unpicked later on and results in the child feeling more confused and worried.

- Say things like, 'They were so special and good that they were needed in heaven.' The child may then fear being good.

- Say, 'Death is darkness and nothingness.' They may then start fearing the dark.

- Say, 'Emily has gone to sleep.' They may fear sleeping.

- Say, 'Bradley has gone on a long journey.' They may think they have been abandoned and/or that Bradley will return from that trip one day.

What to say to a griever

- Remember there are no perfect words.

- So many people avoid speaking to someone who has just experienced a loss. Talking to them (whatever you say) is so much better than not talking to them.

- Asking 'How are you feeling?' will typically elicit the automatic response of 'I'm fine,' when they obviously aren't. If someone does tell you they are doing well, try not to affirm this, as it is often a front on their part. By confirming that they are 'fine' you can lock them into a feeling that if/when they do fall apart they will be letting others down.

- Often just being near someone, a few quiet words and a hug and so on is all that is initially needed. Grievers tend to remember those people who were around them in the early days supporting them, rather than remembering the specific words that were said.

- Often the best rule is 'Show up, shut up and listen (with your ears and your heart).'

- It's by talking – the telling of stories and memories – that the griever begins the grieving process and this leads to healing. *So don't focus on what to say, focus on listening.*

Helpful things you can say include:

- 'I'm here for you.'
- 'I'm sorry for your loss.'
- 'Take all the time you need.'
- 'I wish I had the perfect words, but just know I care.'
- 'My favourite memory of [name] is [memory].'
- *Just be with the person.*

What not to say to a griever

Try to avoid clichés and common platitudes such as the following.

- 'Time heals.' (Time doesn't always heal all wounds, although healing does take time.)
- 'Try to look for the positive.'
- 'Your friend is in a better place.' (There is no better place than them being with you.)
- 'Try not to cry, [name] wouldn't want you to cry.' (This will only stifle the person's emotions.)
- 'I know how you feel.' (You can never really know how someone feels; saying this will probably make the griever angry.)
- 'At least s/he is no longer in pain.' (But the griever is still in pain.)
- 'Don't cry! It will upset your friends/teacher/father/mother/ siblings.' (This creates a sense of guilt for the griever and the burden of having to manage other people's emotions as well as their own.)
- 'There is a reason for everything.'
- 'Be strong.'
- 'If you think this is bad, I know a family who…' (Do not compare or minimise losses.)

Mind, Body and Spirit

CHAPTER 20

How Emotions and Grief Affect the Body and the Breath

Max Strom said in his book, *A Life Worth Breathing*: 'To develop the breath is to open the door to transformation…what most people don't realise is that the nervous system can be brought into harmony through breathing techniques and with zero side effects' (Strom, 2010, p.101).

Have you ever thought about how your emotions affect your body and your breathing? Let's stop, take a breath and give it some consideration.

We have probably all experienced the effects of having a big bawling cry. Our breathing becomes difficult and laboured, our face flushes, our body convulses and we feel completely exhausted. This is a very clear and strong demonstration of how our emotions affect our body and our breath.

Grief is a normal and healthy response to loss and it affects the 'whole' person and the 'whole' body.

With grief there are many subtle ways that our body is affected. When we are in shock over a death we tend to be operating on adrenaline and our breathing becomes much shallower. The bereavement and stress of the loss also leads us to hold tension in our body, especially the face, neck and shoulders.

These 'physical symptoms of grief' all make it much more difficult (if not impossible) for a bereaved child to focus in class and be engaged in learning. It is also extremely difficult for staff who are experiencing these symptoms of grief to carry out their job effectively.

However, these symptoms can all be improved and alleviated with a few very simple techniques.

Breath awareness

1. Sit in a relaxed posture (legs hip width apart, feet flat on the floor, shoulders down, head central) or lie on the floor (flat on your back, in a straight line, with your arms at your sides and legs slightly apart).

2. Slowly breathe in through your nose to a count of four, ensuring that you are breathing deeply into your stomach, filling your diaphragm.

3. Now release the breath slowly through your nose, again to a count of four.

4. Repeat this four times.

5. Next, try to breathe in for a count of four, but out for a count five (repeat four times).

6. When you can do this without effort, breathe in for a count of four and out for a count of six (repeat four times). Only increase the length of your out-breath if it is comfortable for you to do so.

Deepening your in-breath and extending your out-breath in this way will have an immensely relaxing effect, allowing your body and all of its muscles to relax completely. It will dissolve tension and have a calming effect on your mind and all the emotions that are swirling around within it.

This simple breath awareness can be taught to adults and children (and it's not just beneficial during bereavement; it's helpful at any time of high emotions, stress or anxiety).

For some children it will be possible to teach them this breathing technique with simple words/pictures/symbols/sign supports and demonstrations. However, children who are more severely disabled may need to discover this breathing technique through you – by being close to you when you are practising it yourself. In this situation it is best to have the children lying on the floor with you (or for you to be very close to them in their chair/wheelchair). Adults need to work one-to-one with a child (with each child being supported by the adult they best connect with) and ensure that they have lots of eye contact with the child (as long as the child is comfortable with eye contact; this may be difficult with some children who have ASD). Exaggerate your breathing (in and out) so the child can see what you're doing. If the child is happy for you to do so, take their hand and place it on your stomach to feel the breath filling your abdomen. Then place their hand under your nose to feel the air coming out. Finally (again, only if they are happy to do so), do the same with their hand on their stomach and under their nose.

Having soft, relaxing music playing in the background often helps a great deal when doing this kind of work. (There is more on the use of music in Chapter 21.)

> Many of us have fear about breathing deeply because we know deep down that our breath is somehow connected to our emotions. If we are stressed out and besieged with unexpressed grief, rage or fear, then deep breathing terrifies us. So, we keep our breaths small and shallow and erratic. (Strom, 2010, p.106)

Holistic Support

There are many holistic ways in which we can support children with their grief. A teacher who can think creatively and employ a wide range of supportive techniques and mechanisms will be far more likely to support a child with their bereavement successfully.

Using the arts

The arts provide us with many excellent tools to develop learning and understanding with our children. This applies across the curriculum and includes bereavement and grief work.

The arts are accessible to all and are very immediate in nature. Through drawing, painting, movement, music and dance, the children are able to express themselves from the very first brush stroke, arm movement or beat of the drum.

Art, music and movement are all activities that do not rely on language but still have the power to elicit a great deal of expression and emotion. These types of activities take the pressure of having to talk about the loss away from verbal children and are also very accessible for non-verbal children.

For children who do not have language or have limited language, the arts provide a different means of communicating their grief. This can also be of great use for children with verbal skills; when words seem inadequate or they are tired of talking they can instead express themselves through art.

The creative arts are also a very safe and secure place to explore thoughts and feelings. They are a mechanism to bypass a cognitive response to a loss and instead engage the subconscious emotions, which helps assist the child in making sense of the loss.

The use of the creative arts in supporting grieving children is only ever limited by the teacher's level of creative thinking. (See Appendix D for examples of creative arts lessons.)

Using Intensive Interaction

The Intensive Interaction Institute (2016) states that: 'Intensive Interaction is an approach to teaching the pre-speech fundamentals of communication to children and adults who have severe learning difficulties and/or autism and who are still at an early stage of communication development.'

Intensive Interaction is an excellent approach to use with children who have SLD or PMLD. For children who are non-verbal or who have limited verbal skills, Intensive Interaction provides a meaningful connection with others and the ability to express themselves in a very profound way.

In its simplest terms, Intensive Interaction takes place when a child and an adult sit (or whatever position is most comfortable for the child) close together and whatever noise and/or movement the child makes, the adult copies.

The child quickly sees that they are making something happen. Whenever they do something, it is copied; they are in control of the interaction. This repetition and reinforcement of their sounds and movements – the back and forth of the exchange – is a conversation.

When Intensive Interaction is an integral part of a child's learning programme, it not only helps them to develop early language skills, but also gives them greater confidence and empowers them to express their emotions and feelings.

What adult hasn't made a guttural sound to express their frustration rather than using words, finding this expression of feeling far more beneficial than verbal language? When a child doesn't have words to express themselves their sounds, movements, facial expressions and body language help to do this. And when we as adults take the time to listen to these subtle modes of communication and repeat them back to the child, it not only shows that we are listening, but also shows that we care and validates the child's thoughts and emotions. This is an incredibly powerful tool when supporting a grieving child and one I cannot recommend highly enough.

Important things to remember when using Intensive Interaction

- The adult and child need to have a very close working relationship.

- You need to give the child time to communicate.

- Don't be afraid to wait *many* minutes for the child to make a noise and/or a movement.

- Copy the sounds and/or movement as closely as possible.

- Repeat sounds and movements back to the child as soon as they have finished making them.

- Put aside all of your fears of embarrassment. What you are doing may not be the 'norm', but do you think the child looks silly when they make the sound? No, of course not – we praise them for making an utterance. And when a baby is in the very early stages of learning to talk and making different gurgling sounds, we all love to mimic these. So forget about what anyone else might think and just go for it. For if you don't fully engage in the act of Intensive Interaction and respond to the child, it's like ignoring a friend when they are talking to you. You will also learn so much about the child from having these wonderful exchanges with them.

Non-verbal communication, such as Intensive Interaction, provides the bereaved child with another means to help cope with an overwhelming situation.

Massage

Anyone who has had a massage understands the therapeutic power of touch. A good massage eases away your physical and emotional tensions, leaving you feeling relaxed and emotionally lighter.

If your school employs the use of massage in children's learning programmes, increasing the frequency of massage for a bereaved child would be very wise.

If your school doesn't currently use massage as part of its curriculum, it is definitely worth considering.

Why use massage?

- It is a form of communication.

- It is a bonding tool.

- It stimulates the body's muscles and internal organs.

- It develops self-esteem.
- It promotes relaxation.
- It helps to calm the body and mind.

'Touching is the first communication a baby receives and the first language of its development is through the skin' (Leboyer, 1997, p.126).

In-house counselling

Many schools have their own trained counsellor; a member of staff who is trained in a child counselling programme. If you are fortunate enough to have such an excellent resource, then following a death in the school community you should look at increasing the amount of time this person has each week to provide counselling to affected children. You should also look carefully at who needs this counselling most and prioritise the counsellor's time accordingly.

Not all sessions would need to be one-to-one. For some children, a whole-class session would be beneficial, following this up with one-to-one sessions for those children who require it.

If your school doesn't have an in-house counsellor, then following the death you may need to employ the services of one or if you have access to a local authority educational psychologist, request for them to come in and work with affected children.

Peer support

Within your school you may have students who are willing and able to be peer supports to grieving children. You may even already have such a peer support system in place and if this is the case you can use the pairings that are already in operation to help support bereaved children.

These 'peer supports' can act as someone whom the grieving child talks to or can be someone that they spend time with to help them forget about the death. They may like to go for a run with this child when they need time out and a physical release. The possibilities for peer support work are endless.

Think about the connections pupils have across the school and pair pupils up accordingly. You can also be very creative in what these peer supports do with their buddy: artwork, construction, music making, sport, cookery and so on.

Pets as therapy (PAT)

If your school already has access to animals that are trained as PAT, you are in a great position to use these animals as a tool to support bereavement and loss. For the children (and staff) who are grieving, having an animal close by and being able to talk to them or just spend time with them is absolutely wonderful. The giving and receiving of unconditional love to an animal is immensely powerful and supportive. Being able to pet and brush the animal is also very calming and comforting.

If your school doesn't already have PAT or access to PAT it is definitely worth looking into, as the benefits go far beyond just being used with people who are grieving. The benefits of PAT are as follows.

- It is a calming influence.

- It aids physical development – encouraging children to walk with or move towards the animal.

- It helps to get children out into nature – giving the animal a walk, taking care of their hutch and so on.

- Animals are amazing educational tools. Children who struggle to stay on task or lack educational confidence in their abilities are encouraged to focus and work harder by having their trusted pet pal with them.

- It promotes communication – animals communicate well with humans and the humans don't have to be verbal. Non-verbal children will also have a great 'conversation' with the animal.

- Animals develop self-esteem and confidence in the child by providing them with companionship. Children who may have struggled to develop friendships and relationships with others are boosted by the relationship they develop with the animal.

- Animals can support a child's behaviour management programme, for example 'If you complete your maths activity successfully you can take Bruno for a walk.'

- Pets help to teach life skills – having to look after an animal, taking care of its needs and being responsible for it.

- Animals are a therapeutic tool. Children talk and share their problems with the animal. Over time this will result in them opening up with adults too.

- It's fun!

Finally, the things that improve our mood and mental health will also help to improve the mental health of the children who we work with. These might include: spending time outside, being around others, drawing a picture, listening to music and so on. So be creative – there's no limit to the number and type of things that we can do to help our students through the difficult times of bereavement and loss.

CHAPTER 22

Remembering

Special Assemblies and Memorials

When an important person in a child's life dies, having positive memories of that person and taking time to remember them are important parts of the grieving process. The children will no longer have a physical connection with the deceased, but they still have an emotional connection with them. Sharing and exploring memories of the person who has died helps the child to form a sense of why they feel the way they do and why they are grieving.

If a child doesn't attend the funeral or memorial service, then having another way for them to formally say goodbye and mark the life of the deceased is especially important.

There are many ways to remember a person who has died. More formal occasions, such as holding a special assembly at school or having a school memorial service, are good ways to begin the grieving process at school.

How to plan and hold a special assembly or memorial service at school

Not everyone at school will be able to attend the funeral of the person who has died, therefore it is crucial to have a service of some sort at school. It is often good to have an initial assembly very shortly after the school has been informed of the death – at the end of that day or the next day. This allows you to bring the whole school together to acknowledge what has happened and to share feelings, emotions and thoughts.

It is then wise to organise a more 'formal' memorial service at school in which you celebrate the child's life. This service should be very much aimed at the needs of the pupils and the immediate school community, but you may wish to invite the family of the bereaved child or family of the member of the school community who has died. If you do invite the family, let them know what the service will entail, the format and the contents. Also ask them if they would like to play a role in the service or if they just wish to be a part of the audience.

As this special assembly/memorial service is part of the school's grieving process, in my opinion it is best to conduct it as a school event with the parents/carers/family attending should they wish to, rather than them playing a very active role in its planning and delivery.

Pupils should most definitely be involved in the planning and delivery of this service, especially those closest to the child who has died – their class and best friends. If it is a staff member who has died, the children who were closest to this person and who are most affected by the loss should be involved in the service. Encourage these children do the following.

- Choose photos to be shown at the service.
- Choose the music and songs.
- Choose examples of the child's work, favourite toys, etc.
- Share stories, memories and thoughts.
- Decide whether people should be asked to dress up or to wear something special. For example, if the person loved hats, everyone could wear a hat or if their favourite colour was blue, everyone could wear blue.
- If the person was particularly known for something (e.g. a child loving Peppa Pig or a member of staff loving *The Great British Bake Off*), maybe every child in the school could have a Peppa Pig or cake template to colour and decorate. These could then be made into a special display during the assembly/service.
- All children (and staff) should be involved in joining in (to the level that they are comfortable with) with the songs and activities of the service and be given the opportunity to speak: sharing stories, recollections, memories and thoughts.
- Have a 'Remembering [name of the deceased] Box' – a box where thoughts and feelings about the individual can be collected. This should be available during and after the assembly and for

some considerable time thereafter so that children and staff can add their thoughts and feelings when they are comfortable and able to do so. They may not have felt able to stand up and do this during the service or thoughts may not have come to them at that point, but it will be a very important part of their on-going grieving process to share these things. Additions to the box can be named or anonymous. At a later date they can all be collated and shared with the whole school along with the family of the deceased person.

Do not exclude any child who wants to attend such a service/ assembly. Accept that there will be a range of behaviours at such a gathering: tears, disruptions, aggression and so on. Do not dismiss anyone's reactions and do not exclude people who aren't being 'quiet'. Provide times during the assembly when no one is speaking (e.g. sharing photos on a projector) so that it doesn't matter if the assembly hall is noisy with the different reactions and behaviours the children are exhibiting. A special assembly should be organised in a manner that is inclusive to all pupils; no child should be removed from the event unless they present a physical danger to themselves or others.

Remember, the grieving process can be delayed if children are denied the opportunity to participate in 'goodbye rituals' and ceremonies.

In the coming weeks and months after the special assembly or school memorial service, it is good practice to follow it up with activities to help the child remember the person who has died.

Memory activities

- Gathering together photographs of the person who has died and making books about them (that the children can then look at in the coming months and years).

- Putting together DVDs of things that the child did at school: school play, hydrotherapy, sports day and so on. Again, these resources can be a real comfort to look at in the coming months and years.

- Using a piece of fabric from one of the deceased's favourite shirts, dresses, etc. to make a cushion or toy (or simply having a piece of the fabric from this item of clothing for a bereaved child to carry as a memento).

- Making a memory book about the deceased's favourite things. Their favourite colour, food, animal, band, toys, books, pictures and so on.

- Making CDs of their favourite pieces of music, songs, audio stories, etc.

- Creating a visual timeline of the deceased person's life. Use photos, pictures, postcards and even small objects to help remember key events. These can include: starting school, being a bridesmaid, going to London, visiting the zoo and so on.

The Environment

CHAPTER 23

How to Manage the School Environment Following the Death of a Member of the School Community

Following the death of a member of the school community, the atmosphere and mood of the school will undoubtedly be affected. We don't just grieve as individuals; we also grieve as groups, as communities, as schools. Here are some things to consider regarding the school environment that will help members of the school deal with the shock of the death and assist them with the long-term grieving process.

- Your school may want to have a symbol that is put up following the news of a death, something akin to a flag flying at half mast. It could be a large decorative sunflower that is put above the school sign or a large mosaic heart placed by the entrance (whatever motif best fits your school). This symbol communicates to the school community that there has been a bereavement. All members of the school community should already have been informed of this news, but displaying this symbol ensures that everyone entering the building is aware that there has been sad news recently and they can adjust their behaviour accordingly. If they haven't been informed of the death, they can ask at the school's reception. It will probably be appropriate to display this symbol for about a week.

- Have a photo of the deceased person displayed in the entrance of the school. The photo should not be on immediate display as you come into the building so that it is the first thing you see but should be a little further inside. This photo reminds children (and staff) that this person is no longer with us but that we remember her/him. It also serves as a reminder that as a community we are supporting each other.

- Have a beautiful plant, sculpture, vase of flowers or burning (electric) candle next to a photo of the person who has died. If it was a pupil who has died, maybe place one of their favourite toys/resources next to the photo to help emphasise that this is a special memorial for that child.

- Apart from this memorial, keep other parts of the school exactly the same. It is important that the rest of the environment remains as constant as possible for the pupils, as they will have enough to cope with without there being lots of changes to their surroundings.

- In the staffroom have photos of the person who has died so that staff can easily access them and use them in their individual classes to help pupils come to terms with the death.

- Having a framed photo of the deceased in the staffroom is also a good tool to help encourage staff to discuss their thoughts and feelings with each other.

- Ensure that there are plenty of tissues in classrooms, the staffroom, offices and toilets. When people are upset and crying, having to hunt around for tissues is less than ideal.

- Ensure that the staffroom is well stocked with tea, coffee, milk and snacks and that classrooms are well resourced with drinks and snacks for the children. It's bad enough on a 'regular' school day not to have a nice drink and something to eat, but when emotions are high, being able to meet these basic needs easily is crucial.

CHAPTER 24

How to Manage the Classroom Environment Following the Death of a Pupil

My experience has shown me that when a pupil dies, the staff of the class that the child was in will have very different reactions to how and when the child's equipment, resources, name, artwork and so on should be removed from the classroom. What follows is my advice on how best to handle these difficult decisions.

Some staff will want to remove everything related to the child straight away, believing this is the best way to handle the situation, as it will reduce the upset for the rest of the class. In truth, this is just the best way for *them* to cope. Of course, we don't want to neglect our colleagues' feelings concerning the death (and another member of staff should talk to them about how they are feeling), but it really is best, initially, to leave the classroom exactly the same.

In the immediate days following the death of a pupil, the classmates need to begin to understand that the child is no longer with them. Keeping the classroom exactly the same helps to do this. Seeing the child's equipment and resources, such as a standing frame or work chair, empty and unused helps the other children to understand that the person isn't with them anymore.

Having the usual routines at registration, circle time, etc. also reinforces this. For example, go through all the names of the children in the class (including the pupil who has died) in the usual manner. When you get to the deceased child's name, use this as another means of explaining that the child has died and is no longer with us. As explained in Chapter 6, the children will need to be told of the death more than once for it to be taken in and fully understood. You should continue doing this for perhaps a week; it depends on the cognitive level of the children. As the teacher, you will know how long this routine needs to persist for the children in your class to understand that the child is no longer with them.

As we know, transitions are especially difficult for children with SEND, and following the death of a classmate the children have to come to terms with many changes: the loss of a friend and the altered dynamics in the classroom (with special school classes being so much smaller, the loss of one pupil really makes a big difference), along with the changes that come with the removal of the deceased's belongings and resources.

Table 24.1: The approximate timescale for changing the classroom environment

Timescale	When exactly	What to do
When you hear of the death		Keep everything exactly the same.
Week 1	The rest of the week following the news of the death	Keep everything exactly the same.
Week 2	At the end of school on the Friday of Week 1 so that everything is ready for the start of Week 2	Remove the child's equipment such as wheelchairs, work chairs, physiotherapy wedges, etc., including large equipment that was used solely by this child.
At the end of the half term	After school on the last day prior to the school holiday	Remove the child's name labels from pegs, drawers, etc. and all of the remaining individual things belonging to the child. I feel that it is best to leave artwork up until you plan to change the whole display. It is also good to have a photo of the child displayed for the remainder of the school year; this helps the rest of the class to think about and 'talk' about their friend and share their feelings.

At the end of a school week and prior to a school holiday are good times to make changes to the classroom environment so that the pupils come back to a change in the room following a break away from it.

The staff team needs to discuss these changes, how they will be carried out and when they are going to take place so that everyone is prepared and in agreement.

Keep a box with a few of the child's favourite toys, resources, books, etc. plus photos of the child. Use these resources periodically with the class as an aid to help talk about and remember the child who has died. These resources will be key in supporting the ongoing grieving process.

Equipment that has been provided by an external agency such as standing frames from the physiotherapy team can often take a long time to be collected. It is wise to remove the child's name from this piece of equipment and place it in a storage cupboard while it waits to be collected or reallocated.

Other equipment that the child used and that belongs to the school should also have the child's name removed and be cleaned. If it is a chair that had a very distinctive cover and that was very much associated with the deceased child, it is best to use an alternative cover so that you are removing the child's association with it.

Families

CHAPTER 25

How to Support Families

When a school experiences the death of a student or someone close to the school, all of the families are part of the grieving community and the school should play a role in supporting them. Families will look for differing levels of support and as a school you need to be prepared to provide the level of support that each individual family requires.

The family of the deceased child will probably have a tight mechanism supporting them – their close and extended family, friends, medical professionals (hospital or hospice staff), social workers and so on – but this doesn't mean they won't also look to the school for support. The school is the constant and central point of many of our families' lives. Make sure you keep in regular contact with the family after the death so that you can support them as well as signpost them to other support services as required.

Bereaved parents

Following the death of their daughter/son, some parents may wish to retain contact with the school for a long time. The type of contact that they seek could be: occasional phone calls, remaining on the fundraising group for the school, having the school newsletters sent to them, being invited to school events, plays, fetes, etc. You should contact the family every so often to see if they would like you to alter the type or frequency of this contact in any way.

Other families in the school community will look to the school for personal guidance and advice on how to best support their child with the bereavement. Special schools are very close-knit communities and the death of a child will rock many families' lives, especially those where their own child may have a limited life expectancy.

How can a school best support families?

It is vital to inform parents of the death as soon as possible and let them know what information is being shared with the children and what support they will be receiving. Be clear and upfront from the beginning, as this will help to avoid difficult conversations later on.

A letter informing families of the death (see Appendix B for a draft letter) should go home with each child (a paper copy, email or however your school is set up to regularly communicate key information), with telephone calls being made to those parents who have literacy difficulties and those who you know will struggle with hearing the news due to their child currently being unwell, in hospital, etc. (as detailed in Chapter 7).

There should also be different levels of information being shared: basic information for all children and their families and more specific information for the class of the child who has died. This information should detail how the class will be staffed, special activities that will take place, the support and counselling that will be on offer to pupils and so on. Make sure you have template letters covering these areas prepared in advance (see Appendix B for examples of template letters).

You also need to let families know about the funeral arrangements, especially if it is the funeral of a pupil, as this may impact on the school day. In this letter you need to provide information to say whether:

- the family of the deceased child is happy for children to attend the funeral
- the funeral will impact on the school day and staffing for classes and if so how it will be affected, including whether:
  - the whole school will be closed for the day or just part of the day
  - it is just the class of the deceased pupil that will be closed for the day/half day
  - children in this class who want to attend school on that day can be placed in another class.

The specific arrangements for the day of the funeral (if it is a school day) need to be shared with families as soon as possible so that they can decide whether to attend and if they need to make any childcare arrangements. Providing the families with this information will also help them support their child at home with the changes that will take place on the day of the funeral.

It may be relevant to schedule a parent meeting to share with families how the children's loss is being supported at school and to provide advice on what they can do at home to support their grieving child (see Appendix C).

If the death happened at school or involved an infection that was acquired at school (e.g. the child who died had a known medical condition and catching a stomach bug at school led to them deteriorating quickly and dying), these types of circumstances could cause alarm for parents/carers/families and it would be advisable to have a meeting as soon as possible to address all of these issues and concerns.

When a family knows their child is dying

The parents of children with life-limiting conditions will probably have been told at an early stage that their child will die at a young age. When staff are working with families that are in this position, it is important that they balance their conversations. A balance between hope (hope that a cure will be found or medical advances mean they have a longer life than originally predicted) and reality (that they will die at a young age).

Families (and schools) that are open to discussing the fact that someone is dying (including with the person who is dying, as appropriate) tend to be the most effective.

Using your family link worker and school nurse

If your school has a family link worker and/or school nurse, these members of staff will be key in supporting families. Both the family link worker and school nurse will be able to help disseminate information to families.

The family link worker will be able to meet with families who are bereaved, either at their home, school or a neutral environment such as a coffee shop – whatever space the family is most comfortable in. They will not only support the family, but can also signpost them to any other services that they require.

The school nurse can also help with these types of meetings and conversations, if you have both roles within your school then the school nurse will probably be better placed to deal with concerns that other families have about the medical needs of their child. The death of one child will heighten parents' concerns about the health of their own child, especially if their child has a life-limiting condition.

Talk to the families

Following the death of a parent or other key person in a child's life, schools are often nervous about the right thing to do at times such as Mother's Day (when the child's mother has died). Do you include the child in the activity of making a mother's day card but get them to make it for their grandmother? Or do you instead get them to do a different activity? The best thing to do in any situation like this is to *ask the parent/carer/family*. They would much rather be involved and discuss the most relevant and meaningful thing for the child to do (e.g. making a card for the child's aunty, as she has taken on many caregiving roles since the death and has a very strong connection with the child) rather than there be a difficult and awkward situation for everyone involved.

Families coping with trauma

Traumatic events such as a death or a life-altering accident affect us so deeply because they shake our view that the world is a safe and fair place and that there is meaning and significance in all events. As adults, we think that if we are clever and conscientious enough, we can protect ourselves and our children from harm. The death of a child rocks all of these beliefs.

As a school, it is good to remind parents that dealing with a trauma (whatever the nature of the trauma) is something we all tend to have very little experience of. It's not a typical parenting skill, so parents shouldn't give themselves a hard time if they are unsure about how to handle bereavement and grief. The school is there to support them and if the school is only able to help to a certain point, it can then signpost the family to other professionals (counsellors, psychologists, psychiatrists, etc.) for further guidance.

Children's reactions vary immensely and (as with adults) are completely individual. The reason children often recover from a traumatic event more quickly than an adult is because children operate in the now – the immediate present – rather thinking about the past and future. Also, their physical capability to only be able to tolerate intense feelings for short periods of time means they cannot sustain deep grief for an extended duration. Instead, they tend to experience their grief for a brief period and then move away from it until they are able to cope with the intensity again. This can appear to others to be avoidance or denial of the emotions, but instead it is a very effective coping strategy.

Traumas are, of course, devastating. It is our response to traumas, however, that can make it possible to survive them and carry on with our lives. Children will be less affected by a trauma if the adults around them are generally calm and reassuring.

Recovering from trauma is about being able to carry on with life, putting the experience behind us (but not forgetting) and being able to resume daily living. For children, this is all about going back to 'the work' of being a child (playing) – anything that the adults around the child can do to provide an environment that supports this will greatly help the child, for example maintaining routines.

Children will see the trauma in a different manner to the adults. Unlike adults, children do not tend to see the bigger, longer-term implications. On the other hand, if the trauma is the death of a child, the parents will think of the things that the child will not be able to achieve: completing their schooling, getting a boyfriend, leaving home and so on.

Remember that anything (large or small) can trigger emotions related to a trauma, even long after you think you have come to terms with the loss. A film, song, smell, event, etc. can act as a trigger. Being prepared (as far as possible) for these reminders is best, but of course this isn't always possible.

Finally, when people support each other and work together to help each other tackle grief, the grief is easier to manage. To achieve this, adults need to be open and willing to talk to children about death and loss. Schools and families that foster and share this ethos will help tremendously.

Special Days

CHAPTER 26

Anniversaries

When a person who was close to us dies, anniversaries and special events can be very hard. Birthdays, Christmas and the anniversary of the death are all times when we tend to particularly remember the person and it can feel as if we are experiencing the loss all over again.

On the first anniversary of a death, it is advisable for the school to take some time to think about the person who has died. If the death was a pupil then the class the child was in should also do something special together, such as an activity that the deceased enjoyed, for example a session in the hydrotherapy pool, baking or a trip to the park. Making a memory lantern or looking through photo albums and the memory box (see Chapter 11) are also good ways to mark the day and help with the long-term grieving process.

If the death only affects one child, for example a pupil marking the anniversary of the day their father died, then the school should talk to the family about how the day should be marked at school and the best ways that the school can support the anniversary. This may also be a good time to discuss with the family how the child is coping in general. Some families may ask that nothing in particular is done during the school day, as the family will be doing something special together in the evening or at a later date. If this is the case, staff still need to be prepared that the child may want to talk more about their father on this day and that the child's emotions may be heightened, as they are aware of the significance of the day (having picked up on the emotions and conversations of their family).

The anniversary of a death is a reflective day, often with moments of sadness, but on the whole this should be a day (if at all possible) to remember the happy times that were had with the deceased – a day where the bereaved child (or the wider school population if the death affected a class or the entire school) has a special time with their friends and together they move a little further through the grieving process.

If the anniversary relates to the death of a pupil, member of school staff or someone close to the school community then the need for marking the day is just as important for staff in the school as it is for the pupils. They, too, will need to acknowledge the significance of the day and in turn this will also help them with their grief.

Other special days, such as the person's birthday, should be marked in a similar way as the anniversary of their death. That is, as a day to stop and acknowledge the loss and to remember the good times that you had together.

CHAPTER 27

Having an Annual Event
Friendship Day

Special schools that experience a lot of deaths may wish to have a regular/annual event to mark the lives of children and other members of the school community who have died.

Friendship Day

At one of the schools where I worked, we developed an annual Friendship Day – a day where we celebrated *all friends*: friends who were no longer with us and those who still were. On this day each year, we held a service outside. The service was held in the playground around a tree that was planted in memory of a member of staff who had died.

If a pupil or member of the school community had died in the past year, we thought about that child or adult, remembered something very distinctive about them and created something in response (e.g. if they loved butterflies, each child in the school would make a decorative butterfly). If the person loved wearing something in particular, for example badges or the colour yellow, we might have all worn a badge or a yellow item of clothing.

The family of the person who had died was invited to the service (but they were in no way obliged to attend – they would only come if it was right for them to do so). If they did attend, they were asked if they wished to say anything or be directly involved in any way. All of the families, friends and supporters of the school were also invited to attend Friendship Day.

During the service we sang 'friendship songs', read poems and generally celebrated those we loved and had a very happy and uplifting experience.

Following the service everyone went into the school for refreshments or they were enjoyed outside if the weather was good.

The students in the sixth form held a regular coffee shop for the school and local community so they were excellent at hosting this event. Drinks and snacks were enjoyed together, helping to further develop our friendships and connections with each other whilst also thinking and talking about friends who we missed. Lots of lovely memories and happy stories were shared on this day.

In the afternoon the school had a disco for all of the pupils. This was another great way for friendships to be fostered across the school.

All in all this annual event was a very happy and positive day and a day that experience has shown really helped pupils, families and staff come to terms with the death of members of the school community.

Other regular/annual events you may wish to do at your school include:

- planting a tree in memory of a child who has died
- developing a sensory flowerbed and adding new plants or ornaments to it when a pupil dies with each item having a name plaque of the person that it is in memory of
- having a special gallery of photos of friends who are no longer alive – a corridor or space in the school with a framed photo of each person who has died
- releasing balloons when a child or member of the school community has died – pupils in the school can write thoughts or memories of the person on tags that are then attached to the balloons.

School Management

CHAPTER 28

School Bereavement and Loss Policy

As previously discussed, it is imperative that every school has a bereavement and loss policy (see Chapter 4). Below is information to help you through the process of writing this policy. Ideally, you need to cover each of the bullet points below. (In Appendix A you will find a draft bereavement and loss policy.)

Framework for developing a school bereavement and loss policy

Introduction

- Why you need this policy.

- How supporting bereavement and loss fits in with the school ethos.

- The date the policy was written and by whom.

Aims

- The policy should give all pupils and staff faced with a bereavement or loss the support they need and in a manner that is appropriate to them.

Key people in supporting this policy

- Key coordinator. *This is usually the headteacher.*

- The 'Crisis Team'. *The usual members of a Crisis Team are: the headteacher, deputy headteacher, business manager/other senior member of the administration team, school nurse, school leader in charge of pastoral issues.*

Roles and responsibilities

- The role of: class teachers, school nurse, educational psychologist, counsellor, etc.

Procedures

Procedures for (rather than including these in the policy document and it becoming too large, you may only want to reference these procedures in the policy and have the full details in a separate procedures document):

- the funeral
- long-term illness
- the death of a pet
- support for bereaved children
- support for parents and families
- responding to the media.

(See Chapter 29 for information on these procedures.)

Staff support and training

- Provide an outline of the bereavement and loss training to be provided to staff.

Make sure your school has had training before an event. Training triggered by a death is still good training, but it would be easier to deliver and receive this information when staff are not in the midst of a 'crisis'.

Teaching and learning

- How the school's curriculum teaches about life and death.

Confidentiality

- How information will be shared and confidentiality maintained.

Inclusion and equality

- How different cultural and religious customs and activities related to death will be represented and explained.

Equality, safeguarding and equal opportunities statement

- How the policy will promote equality of opportunity for students and staff from all social, cultural and economic backgrounds and ensure freedom from discrimination on the basis of membership of any group including gender, sexual orientation, family circumstances, ethnic or national origin, disability (physical or mental) or religious or political beliefs.

Links to other policies

- This policy needs to be linked to other guidance and policies including: curriculum, health and safety, and medical policies and those from the local authority and Department for Education, etc.

Monitoring and evaluation

- The date this policy will be reviewed and the reviewer's name should be included, along with how any changes to the policy will be disseminated.

School Bereavement and Loss Procedures

The previous chapter included the areas that a school needs to include in their bereavement and loss policy. This chapter will look at more specific and detailed procedures that it would be very wise to have covered in your school. You may not want to include these in your bereavement and loss policy in case the policy becomes too large, but you could include a reference in the policy to where these procedures can be found.

A school that has well-defined procedures for managing bereavement and loss will, without doubt, have improved outcomes for their grieving students.

Crisis Team

The usual members of a Crisis Team are: headteacher, deputy headteacher, business manager/other senior member of the administration team, school nurse and school leader in charge of pastoral issues.

Various roles need to be assigned within the Crisis Team.

- *Role of communication*: with staff, pupils, families, governors, the wider school community, emergency services, press/media (as appropriate), medical teams and authorities (including Health and Safety Executive and Public Health England regarding any infectious diseases).

- *Role of liaison*: with the affected family/families.

- *Role of troubleshooting:* resolving any issues related to the school site following the death, especially if the death occurred at school: repairs, maintenance and so on.

Depending on the size of your school and the nature of the crisis, you may need to subdivide each role, for example with the role of communication, have one member of the team leading on communication with staff, pupils, families and governors and another member of the team dealing with communication with the wider school community, emergency services, press/media (as appropriate), medical teams and relevant authorities.

Procedures – from being informed of the death through to the funeral

1. Make sure that the Crisis Team is in place and everyone knows what their role is and what they have to carry out.

2. Inform staff and governors of the death.

3. Tell pupils of the death.

(In the immediate days after the death, students and staff may require time to come to understand the death and process the loss. The school needs to make arrangements to ensure that there is time and space to do this. This may involve getting in some supply staff and designating a particular room as a 'time-out space'.)

4. Tell the wider school community, including families, other professionals and so on.

5. Contact parents who may require extra support with the news of the death.

6. Inform any necessary authorities (such as the Health and Safety Executive and Public Health England regarding any infectious diseases, etc.).

7. Organise information (letters, etc.) to be shared with parents (see Appendix B).

8. At the start of the day (after the death has been announced), have an initial whole-school staff meeting (further details about this meeting are below) to share further information about the death and to give direction on what should happen that day (e.g. a special circle time to take place in each class, the affected class to go out for a walk or have a swim session).

9. Discuss any at-risk students and put support and intervention plans in place for them.

10. Organise resources to be shared with parents to help them support their child at home (see Appendix C).

11. Ask staff/class teams whether anyone would like assistance in supporting their class or a particular student in processing/ understanding the death. Schedule times to do this.

12. The leadership team needs to be around the school – in the corridors, popping into classes, out on the playground, etc. – to check the mood of the school and provide extra support wherever it is needed.

13. All staff should model appropriate responses to grief and be good grief role models for pupils.

14. Set in motion extra support mechanisms: in-house counselling, peer-to-peer support and external counselling.

15. The Crisis Team should assess the plans, procedures and timeframes and update them as necessary.

16. Plan and lead an after-school (after day one) debrief meeting (further details about this meeting are below).

17. Send a condolence card to the family.

18. Keep in contact with the family.

19. Some staff will request to attend the funeral and you need to have clear policies and procedures outlining who can attend. Unless you decide to close the school for the funeral (which may set a precedent for future funerals), you still need to have a safe level of staffing for the rest of the school. A possible rule for who attends the funeral of a pupil could be staff from the class affected can attend the funeral (if they wish to) and the headteacher (or another representative of the leadership team).

20. Inform the parents of the class (where school staff will be attending the funeral) that the staff will be out of school and for how long. Give parents the choice of keeping their child at home for the period of time that staff will be at the funeral or sending their children into school as normal and, when staff have to leave for the funeral, the children will be placed with another class or have different staff with them.

Initial meeting (following the death) with staff – what to cover

- Share information regarding the death.

- Discuss how to share this information with classes (have copies of Chapters 8 to 14 of this book ready to pass to staff).

- Present information on how children grieve and give an overview of the types of behaviours and questions they might have.

- Review the plan for the current school day and the remainder of the school week, make any necessary changes that might be required.

- Emphasise the need for stability and providing as much normality as possible. Children like and need their routines, but at the same time you need to allow for flexibility – time for when the children want to talk about the death or simply come together and be close and reassured.

- Provide time for discussing the strategic plan for supporting the loss – ensure staff feel able to add suggestions and make changes.

- Plan a 'safe space' where students can go and be alone/quiet (but still be monitored).

- Plan for extra supply staff to be available to take over in any classes where a member of staff needs some time away from the pupils or to provide extra support to classes that need it.

- Allow time for staff to discuss their thoughts and feelings about the death – *this is vital*. Staff need to process the loss and grieve, too.

- Decide on a member of staff to be the family liaison (for the family of the child who has died), as well as someone to act as the point of contact for answering other families' questions – this could be each class teacher or headteacher, etc.

Meeting at the end of the first day – what to cover

- This debrief meeting at the end of the first day should last no more than 30 minutes.

- It allows you to see how things are across the school and how staff are doing. Such get-togethers help develop unity. The more opportunities there are to talk, the better it is for staff (although some may reject this and after a difficult day will be emotionally drained and just need to go home).

- Reiterate that the Crisis Team members are always available for staff to come and talk to.

- Review the day.

- Take the opportunity to discuss the children's reactions. Which children need to be closely monitored? Is there a need for any referrals at this point? (In the coming weeks and months, keep coming back to this question.)

- Which strategies for handling the day, sharing the news, supporting the grief, etc. were most successful?

- Share resources for use with the children – these need to be photocopied and prepared ahead of the meeting and ready to hand to each teacher.

- Plan for the following day/rest of the week, including having an assembly the next day (if this hasn't taken place on day one) to talk about the child who has died.

- Share tips, resources, etc. on how staff can look after themselves and support each other (see Chapters 17–19). These can also be photocopied and handed out to staff.

- Allow staff time to reminisce and tell stories about the child who has died; this is all part of supporting staff grief.

- Make sure staff go home early.

At the next regular staff meeting – what to cover

- Discuss the funeral – who will attend, the logistics of this and how staffing will be managed.

- Discuss how the children are coping. Is there anyone who needs close monitoring? Is there a need for any referrals?

- Discuss and plan for an in-school memorial, special assembly, etc. (see Chapter 22).

- Look again at the resources and ideas for how to support children with grief.

- Revisit the tips, resources, etc. for how staff can look after themselves and support each other (see Chapters 17–19).

It's often good to have a bit of time set aside at the upcoming regular staff meetings to check in on how staff and children are handling the loss; to see if extra support is needed or if any referrals to outside agencies are required.

Being asked to speak at the funeral

As the headteacher or teacher of a pupil who has died, you may be asked to speak at a child's funeral. Although this request can be daunting, it is also a request that you should be immensely proud to have received. The family are acknowledging the important role that you played in their child's life.

I have been asked to speak at several children's funerals and each time I have felt incredibly honoured to have been involved in the formal goodbye of the child. This is not to say, however, that each funeral hasn't been difficult. Below are some tips on how you can prepare for speaking at a pupil's funeral that I hope will make things a little easier for you.

- Talk to the family about what they wish you to say. Would they like you to speak about the child's life and experiences at school, share photos or read a poem or a story?

- If you are going to talk specifically about the child's life and experiences at school, take time to reflect personally and spend time speaking to the pupils and your colleagues to get their thoughts and memories of the child.

- Once you have gathered ideas for your eulogy, make sure that what you write is sincere and personal, using your own words. You will be the person standing at the front of the congregation and you need to be totally comfortable with the words you say.

- As the child's headteacher or teacher, you will have a close relationship with the parents. This connection will help you determine the tone that your eulogy should take.

- Ask the parents if they would like to read what you plan to say at the service in advance.

- Often, parents like to have photos of the child shown at the funeral, either printed in the order of service or displayed on a screen. Taking time to gather together photos of the child will be useful not only if the family asks for these to be used at the funeral, but also for part of your own memorial service in school. (Regardless of whether they are used at the funeral, I always have the collection of photos made into a professionally bound photo book to give to the parents/carers/family.)

- I have always found it useful to have a bottle of 'Rescue Remedy' in my bag when speaking at a funeral. For me, a couple of squirts of Rescue Remedy helps to calm the nerves.

- Prior to speaking at the funeral, take time to do some deep, conscious breathing (as described in Chapter 20). This will help to steady your emotions.

- When you are speaking at the funeral, looking directly at the family of the deceased might be difficult and perhaps even overwhelming for you – doing so may result in you breaking down in tears. Looking slightly above the congregation at the beginning of your eulogy will help you to control your emotions, and then looking at your colleagues will give you the support and confidence to carry on. However, if you are able to speak some of your words directly to the family, I'm sure they will greatly appreciate this personal connection.

Advice on visiting a dying pupil

When it is known that a child is dying and sadly they do not have much time left, the parents of the child may ask if staff members would like to visit them (at home, in hospital or at a hospice, etc.). By doing this, the parents are acknowledging the important role that the school and the people who teach and care for their child have in their lives and their child's life. The parents may also be asking you to visit as they themselves are in need of your support.

Some members of staff may, understandably, want to see the child one last time, and doing so may help them to cope with the death in the longer term. As a school, there are a number of things that you first need to consider, and you should have each of these covered in your bereavement and loss procedures so that you are not left in a difficult position at a very emotional time.

- If you allow a member of staff to visit the dying child during the school day, this person won't be in school doing their regular job. How will the rest of the school cope? Are you compromising the needs of the other pupils?

- By allowing one person to visit during the school day, you are putting yourself in the position that other members of staff could then ask to visit. Potentially the entire team of staff that works with the student may wish to visit, which is clearly completely unmanageable for a school.

- What position are the members of staff going to be putting themselves in if they do visit the child? Could they find themselves having to support family members, explaining things to friends and family, etc.? Are they in a position/able to do this? As the staff member is visiting in 'school time', the family may see this as their role and it could become a rather difficult and complex situation.

- If it is felt that the family needs the support of the school during the school day, I feel that it is best for the family link worker or the school nurse to do this.

- If parents have said that staff members are welcome to come and say their 'goodbyes' to the child, this may be best done outside of school hours to make a clear distinction between this being something that the individual wants to do personally rather than it being a part of their job.

Long-term illness
If a pupil or a member of staff has a long-term illness, the school should assign a person to get in touch with the pupil/member of staff and their family to see what contact they would like from the school (visits, telephone calls, emails, texts and so on) and how regularly they would like to receive this communication.

The named member of staff should also ensure that they are kept informed of any changes and developments (both positive and negative) of the pupil/member of staff's condition in a manner that does not cause distress to the individual or their family.

The named member of staff should share the pupil/member of staff's and their family's wishes with the rest of the school staff.

Death of a pet

Schools should recognise that the death of a pet can be very traumatic for a student and should be treated as any other loss would be.

A pet is very often a member of the family and so its death can be felt as keenly as that of a human. Therefore, support and care should be given in exactly the same manner as it would be for any other type of bereavement.

Many children with SEND have strong attachments to their pets. Some may have a 'therapeutic animal' and the loss of this animal will be felt immensely – they will have lost a key part of how they engage with the world and with others.

Support for bereaved children

Most bereaved children can be supported by school staff and will not require specialist professionals.

The school should support bereaved pupils by:

- providing a caring and supportive environment where pupils know that it is safe for them to express their grief
- providing a routine, familiarity and a sense of normality
- giving the child time and space away from a possibly difficult and emotionally charged home environment (if the death relates to a family member having died)
- providing access to a 'safe space' to be away from the classroom and have time 'alone' to grieve
- having a named member of staff to support the child
- relevant school staff having the time to work with the bereaved child and support them with their grief

- making sure that the bereaved child knows they can express their grief and it won't upset anyone

- providing the opportunity for them to be 'children' – to play and to be with friends – without feeling guilty

- providing regular contact between school and home, and home and school, to provide information and reassurance about how the child is doing

- providing access to the school counsellor, music therapy and any other relevant school resources

- regularly monitoring the child and, if necessary, making a referral to an external professional (following discussion with the family)

- supporting the pupil with ways to remember and commemorate the person who has died.

Support for staff

The school should support members of staff by:

- recognising that staff may, at times, find it challenging to support children who are grieving and providing support to help them manage their feelings

- providing informal times when staff can talk about and share memories of the member of the school community who has died and also discuss their feelings and reactions to the death

- acknowledging that staff who are personally bereaved will also need time and support to manage the bereavement

- giving staff time to attend the funeral if appropriate (make sure that your school has separate school guidance for attending personal funerals, as well as the procedures for who will attend the funeral of a member of the school community, as outlined earlier in this chapter)

- providing bereavement and loss training

- making an up-to-date set of resources available to staff on how to manage personal grief and how to support pupils with bereavement and loss.

Support for parents, carers and families

Schools can support parents, carers and families by doing the following things:

- Immediately contact the family of the deceased and offer support.

- Provide information about the death to members of the school community and others who work with the family, to the level that the family of the deceased wishes to share.

- Contact all families in the school and offer support and advice on how to manage a bereavement with their children.

- Send a card or letter of condolence to the family.

- If the family are in agreement, organise for a representative(s) to attend the funeral.

- Have a collection for flowers (or charity donation, etc.) for the funeral – in line with the family's wishes.

- Invite the parents/carers/family of the deceased to join the school for commemorative events, both following the death and in subsequent years.

- Ensure that support for the parents/carers/family continues for as long as they wish it to.

Responding to the media

There may be occasions when a death or a traumatic situation attracts media attention. In this situation, all members of staff should be told *not* to respond to journalists' questions and enquiries and instead to tell them to contact the headteacher (or the relevant member of the Crisis Team). The headteacher or member of the Crisis Team should then provide a well-thought-through response (having sought further advice, if necessary).

On-going school organisation

Leaders of schools are excellent at acknowledging the different skills, qualifications and experience of their members of staff and making sure they get the maximum benefit for their pupils. This can at times result in small teams of staff working together for a considerable numbers of years. Initially this may not be a problem, but if the area of expertise is working with individuals with medical needs and life-limiting conditions, these members of staff are going to be at the forefront of managing pupil bereavements.

If your school unfortunately regularly experiences pupil deaths, it is wise to make sure that staff do not stay in this type of class for too long. The cumulative impact of multiple pupil deaths on staff members can be tremendous, and this is on top of the on-going daily stress of managing difficult medical situations.

A good school ensures that its staff are trained to be able to work in a wide range of classes with staff who are skilled in multiple areas. This idea of 'burn out' doesn't just apply to staff who are managing medical needs and pupil deaths; it is also relevant to colleagues who are handling complex behavioural issues. All staff need to have changes in where they work in a school to provide interest, new experiences and learning opportunities, and to ensure that a high level of staff wellbeing is achieved.

CHAPTER 30

The Curriculum

Children are never too young to talk about death, so make the most of any appropriate opportunity that arises to discuss life and death. It will gradually build up their understanding and make handling a loss a little easier when it occurs.

A school curriculum that embeds the teaching of life, death and loss across its subjects and across all year groups will, without doubt, help to support children with bereavements and losses that they experience later in life. Children need to develop an understanding of what life and death are before they can accept and manage their own feelings of loss and grief.

Covering issues of life and death across subjects in the curriculum in all year groups provides the perfect incremental approach to learning about life and death, from the start of school and throughout a child's formal education. This approach will build a child's understanding of what alive and dead mean, in terms of wildlife, nature and humans.

The school curriculum also needs to develop the understanding that we can grieve for a wide range of things in life (not just when someone dies), such as grief related to traumas, relationships, loss of belongings and so on.

A curriculum that provides a growth in understanding of life and death will lead toward the children gaining a personal and emotional understanding of what grief is. As we know, knowledge is power and the knowledge that children acquire about death and loss through their schooling will equip them with the tools that they require when they undoubtedly experience grief later in life.

It is very important that the signs, symbols and objects of reference for death, dying and loss are included in the curriculum. They need to be introduced and taught to pupils throughout their time at school, rather than children having to learn them when they are in the midst of a difficult situation and struggling to communicate their grief. Introduce the signs, symbols and objects of reference for death, dying and loss whenever you are talking about death and loss, whether in relation to a plant dying or the loss of a personal belonging. All informal uses of this language will help to familiarise the children with the concepts.

Lessons about life, death and loss should be included across the school curriculum. Subjects where these topics can be taught are: personal, social, health and economic education (PSHE), PE, English, science and history. Below are some ideas of how your school's curriculum can include lessons on life, death and loss.

PSHE

- When learning about our body and how it works, emphasise what the key signs of life are and that when these are no longer present, a person is no longer living: they are dead.

- Teach what different emotions look and feel like, including the physical impact they can have on our body, for example when we cry a lot we can get very hot and tired.

- When learning about emotions, include the emotions associated with grief. At an early age this can be a child's emotional reaction to the death of a pet, their favourite tree in the park dying, flowers dying in the garden in winter and so on.

- Explore the feelings and emotions related to when we lose something special to us or when it breaks/stops working, for example a favourite toy, special bag, jewellery or mobile phone.

PE

- When the children have been exercising vigorously and they experience their heart rate increasing and feel out of breath, talk about the breath and heart rate. Explain that all of these things mean we are alive. When we stop breathing, when our heart stops beating, we are no longer alive: we are dead.

English

- When reading works of fiction and non-fiction and someone or something (animal, plant, etc.) dies, do not gloss over this. Use it is as a discussion point for what alive and dead mean. Reinforce that when someone dies, they cannot be brought back. Stories that talk of monsters coming back to life are just that – stories, fiction, make-believe – and children need to know that this cannot happen when a person dies in real life.

- When the topic of death occurs, talk and write about the emotions that are felt by the people/characters in the stories, poems, news articles and so on.

- Read poems and stories (and encourage children to write their own) about how you feel when you lose something special, for example when your best friend moves away, you break up with your girlfriend, you lose your favourite jacket or your laptop breaks.

- Explore the language of death, grief and loss – look at condolence cards, death announcements in newspapers and so on. Make a list of the different words and phrases that are used and think about whether you and the pupils feel these are the best words to use. If euphemisms are used in the cards, explain to the children what these really mean and come up with your own simpler and clearer phrases.

Science

- When learning about the life cycles of animals, insects and plants, etc. look at and discuss what they each look like and how they behave when they are alive and also when they are dead.

- Build on the PE lessons by learning more about how our bodies work, what they look and feel like when they are working well and what happens when they aren't working so well, including when we are ill and need help from doctors, nurses, hospitals, etc. Sensitively explain that sometimes ill health or an accident can mean that a person's body is 'broken' to a point that even though the doctors and nurses do all that they can to help, they are sometimes unable to make the person better and sadly they die.

History

- When different historical figures are covered in history lessons, you can also talk about how and when they died so that children realise that these 'big names in history' don't have superpowers that allow them to go on living forever; they are humans just like us.

Finally, whenever any incidental life, death and loss learning opportunities occur, for example a pupil has a new baby brother, someone's pet hamster dies, the class iPad is lost and so on, make the very most of these situations. These real-life experiences provide a great vehicle for developing the children's knowledge and understanding of what life, death and loss mean. Endeavour to explore each of these opportunities with your class; sometimes this will be a brief talk at circle time and at other times a more detailed lesson will be appropriate, but each and every one of these fulfilled opportunities goes towards developing the children's concepts of life, death and loss and how to manage the emotions associated with each.

CHAPTER 31

Staff Training

This book has sought to provide you with a framework for staff bereavement and loss training.

The important thing for schools to realise is that bereavement and loss training cannot just be delivered once. There will be staff joining your school at regular intervals and all staff need to have this training. Also, staff who remain in your school for many years need to revisit this training regularly. Members of staff may feel that they have had all of the training that they need, but bereavements that they experience at school and in their personal life mean that their coping mechanisms and emotional responses to death and loss alter over time. They will need further support so that they can handle each of these losses.

I would personally recommend that your school has a rolling programme of bereavement and loss training. Include it in your induction programme for your new staff. Have annual training for all staff – just a small amount (one hour approximately) of training each year and 'full' training every three years.

And if a crisis or trauma affects your school, extra support and training can be put in place at any time.

I hope that this book has provided you with the information, resources and confidence to support and train your staff about bereavement and loss. However, if you require extra guidance or would like a bespoke training package, please do get in touch.

Sarah Helton
Email: backpocketteacher@gmail.com
Website: www.backpocketteacher.co.uk
Blog: www.backpocketteacher.wordpress.com
Twitter: @BackPocketTeach

Appendices

Draft Bereavement and Loss Policy

Introduction

Why we need this policy

Sadly, all schools at some point will be affected by a death: the death of a pupil, a member of staff, someone close to the school community or a pupil's family member.

Most adults struggle to know what to say to another adult who is mourning, but when it is a child who is bereaved they often ignore or try to avoid the issue of the death. This can be as a result of fear – that they will do or say the wrong thing – or because they think avoiding the subject protects the child from any extra sadness and distress.

It is our natural instinct to protect children, but trying to protect them from death and the emotions of grief is unwise and unhelpful.

Children who have SEND may communicate their grief differently, but grief is grief, and their grief is just as valid and powerful as anyone else's and must never be overlooked, ignored or forgotten. Doing so will only leave them in a greater state of confusion and, just like anyone whose grief is neglected, this could impact on their emotional and psychological health beyond all measure.

Also include information on:

- how supporting bereavement and loss fits in with the school ethos
- the date the policy was written and by whom.

Aims

This policy aims to:

- provide information and guidance to staff so that any pupils, staff or members of the school community faced with a bereavement or loss are given the support they need and in a manner that is appropriate to them
- outline the range of support mechanisms available to pupils, staff and members of the school community (including parents, carers and the wider family)
- give an overview of the procedures to be deployed by staff following a bereavement.

Key people in supporting this policy

- Key coordinator. *This is usually the headteacher.*
- Members of the 'Crisis Team'. *The usual members of a Crisis Team are: headteacher, deputy head, business manager/other senior member of the administration team, school nurse, school leader in charge of pastoral issues.*

Roles and responsibilities

Key coordinator

- Has overall responsibility for support and liaison in the event of a death or traumatic loss. If the headteacher is absent then the deputy headteacher will take responsibility.

Crisis Team

- Role of communication: with staff, pupils, families, governors, the wider school community, emergency services, press/media (as appropriate), medical teams and authorities (Health and Safety Executive and Public Health England regarding any infectious diseases).
- Role of liaison: with the affected family/families.
- Role of troubleshooting: resolving any issues related to the school site following the death, especially if the death occurred at school; repairs, maintenance, informing outside agencies and so on.

Senior leadership team (SLT)

In most schools, all of the SLT will be involved in the Crisis Team (above) but if yours is a large school with a bigger SLT, then members of the SLT not involved in the Crisis Team should:

- monitor how staff and pupils are coping with the bereavement
- have a regular presence around the school to see how people are doing (pupils, staff, parents and so on) and be available to provide support to these people as required.

Class teachers

- Provide day-to-day support to the children in their class.
- Be available to parents/carers/families of the children in their class and provide initial support (if this becomes more involved, it needs to be referred to the family link worker).
- Provide day-to-day support to the members of staff in their team.

School nurse

- If the death was in any way related to a contagious disease or illness, ensure all appropriate medical protocols are being followed in the school.
- Reassure parents and staff that all medical protocols are being followed.
- If the death is of a pupil, provide reassurance to parents who have a child with a life-limiting condition, as they may feel especially vulnerable.
- Have information available to signpost pupils, parents/carers/families and staff to extra support as required.

Family link worker

- Have information available to signpost pupils, parents/carers/families and staff to extra support as required.

Counsellor

- Provide counselling to individually bereaved pupils.
- 'Assess' who is most in need of counselling following a pupil in the school dying.
- Be prepared to alter their timetable to address the most pressing needs in the school.

Educational psychologist

- Provide additional support and advice to the school.

Procedures

The school has detailed procedures in place for handling:

- funerals
- long-term illness
- death of a pet
- support for bereaved children
- general support for children
- support for parents and families
- responding to the media.

These procedures can be found at: [*name the location of the procedures*]

Staff support and training

The school is committed to ensuring all staff feel confident and skilled in being able to deliver high-quality support to pupils (and other staff) experiencing a bereavement or loss.

All staff have bereavement and loss training and the school ensures that all members of staff are kept up to date with advice and training developments.

Teaching and learning

Our curriculum embeds the teaching of life, death and loss across its subjects and across all year groups.

Covering issues of life and death across subjects in the curriculum and in all year groups provides the perfect incremental approach to learning about life and death, from starting school and throughout a child's formal education. This approach will build a child's understanding of what alive and dead mean, in terms of wildlife, nature and humans.

The school curriculum also develops children's understanding that we can grieve for a wide range of things in life (not just when someone dies), including grief-related traumas, relationships, loss of belongings and so on.

Lessons about life, death and loss will be included across the school curriculum. Subjects where these topics will be taught include: PSHE, PE, English, science and history.

Confidentiality

Although it is important to maintain confidentiality when handling any incident or disclosure, pupils will be made aware that in some situations complete confidentiality cannot be guaranteed. This will help maintain the trust of pupils and parents/carers/families and will ensure that we are only sharing appropriate information and that the level of information shared is kept to a minimum. Sensitive information will only be disclosed internally (and externally with careful thought about the rights and needs of all individuals concerned).

Inclusion and equality

There is a wide range of religious and cultural customs and rituals concerning death and bereavement. The school recognises that families may have varying approaches concerning death and we respect all families' beliefs and practices. We will ensure that pupils and staff are aware of this range of beliefs and practices and instil the need to respect and value them all.

Equality, safeguarding and equal opportunities statement

In all of its policies and procedures, the school will promote equality of opportunity for students and staff from all social, cultural and economic backgrounds and ensure freedom from discrimination on the basis of membership of any group including gender, sexual orientation, family circumstances, ethnic or national origin, disability (physical or mental) and religious or political beliefs.

Links to other policies

This policy needs to be linked to other guidance and policies including: curriculum, health and safety, and medical policies and those from the local authority and Department for Education, etc.

Monitoring and evaluation

- This policy will be reviewed on [date].
- Any amendments made to this policy will be shared with staff, governors and parents/carers/families.

Template Letters

Informing parents/carers of a pupil death

Dear Parents and Carers,

It is with great sadness that I am writing to inform you of the death of [pupil's name], a pupil in [class name]. [Pupil's name] died [insert appropriate details about the death that have been approved by the family for release to the school community].

For those of you who knew [pupil's name], we ask that you remember and celebrate her/his [insert some of the pupil's positive character traits]. For those of you who did not know [pupil's name], we ask that you respect our sadness and support the school community at this difficult time.

Today, your child's teacher told the class of [pupil's name]'s death and they will support the children in the coming days, weeks and months.

All of our teaching staff have been trained in how to support children with bereavements and they are answering the children's questions and helping them come to terms with this sad news. The school's counsellor will also be available to talk with class groups and individual children who are struggling with the news.

It is very difficult for all of us to face the death of a young person and however much we wish to protect our children from sad news, we should not hide the news of a death from them – it is best to explain the facts to them (to the level of their understanding) and answer any and all questions that they have. Children seek reassurance at a time like this and we can do this best with honesty, love and care.

We have enclosed some suggestions that may prove helpful to you as you talk to your child about [pupil's name]'s death. Please feel free to contact the school if you have any issues or concerns that you would like to discuss.

I know you will join me in extending our heartfelt sympathy to [pupil's name]'s family. When we receive information regarding funeral arrangements, I will share the information with you.

Again, please do not hesitate to contact the school on [telephone number] if you have any concerns or questions.

Yours sincerely,

Informing parents/families of the death of a member of staff

Dear Parents and Carers,

It is with great sadness that I am writing to inform you of the death of [member of staff's name]. [Member of staff's name] worked in [class name or position and office in the school]. [Member of staff's name] died [insert appropriate details about the death that have been approved by the family for release to the school community].

For those of you who knew [member of staff's name], we ask that you remember and celebrate her/his [insert some of the member of staff's positive character traits]. For those of you who did not know [member of staff's name], we ask that you respect our sadness and support the school community at this difficult time.

Today, your child's teacher told the class of [member of staff's] death and they will support the children in the coming days, weeks and months.

All of our teaching staff have been trained in how to support children with bereavements and they are answering the children's questions and helping them come to terms with this sad news. The school's counsellor will also be available to talk with class groups and individual children who are struggling with the news.

It is very difficult for all of us to face the death of someone so close to us and however much we wish to protect our children from sad news, we should not hide the news of a death from them; it is best to explain the facts to them (to the level of their understanding) and answer any and all questions that they have. Children seek reassurance at a time like this and we can do this best with honesty, love and care.

We have enclosed some suggestions that may prove helpful to you as you talk to your child about [member of staff's name]'s death. Please feel free to contact the school if you have any issues or concerns that you would like to discuss.

I know you join me in extending our heartfelt sympathy to [member of staff's name]'s family. When we receive information regarding funeral arrangements, I will share the information with you.

Again, please do not hesitate to contact the school on [telephone number] if you have any concerns or questions.

Yours sincerely,

Informing parents/carers of the details of the funeral

Dear Parents and Carers,

I wrote to you on [date of letter] to inform you of the sad news that [name of pupil or member of staff] had died.

[Name of pupil or member of staff]'s family have now made arrangements for the funeral and they have asked that we share these with the school community.

The funeral will take place on [give date and time] at [give place]. The family requests [provide details given to you by the family regarding the funeral, such as: whether it is for family only or all are welcome, whether there is a dress code and information on flowers and collections, e.g. donations to the local hospital].

If the funeral is taking place during school time, you may wish to include the following.

[Name of pupil or member of staff]'s funeral is taking place during school time. If you wish to attend the service with your child, you are of course welcome to do so. Please inform the school office if your child will be absent from school to attend the funeral.

If the funeral is taking place during school time and is for a pupil, you may wish to include the following.

In accordance with our school policy for bereavement and loss [name of class], the class that [pupil's name] was a member of, will be closed on [date of funeral] for the [morning or afternoon as appropriate for the time of the funeral] so that staff members who wish to can attend the funeral. If your child is in [name of class] you can either keep your child at home for the [morning or afternoon as appropriate for the time of the funeral] or they will be welcomed into other class groups for the [morning or afternoon as appropriate for the time of the funeral] session.

Please do not hesitate to contact the school on [telephone number] if you have any concerns or questions regarding these arrangements or if you would like to discuss how your child is coping with the bereavement.

Yours sincerely,

Inviting parents/carers/families of the deceased pupil to a memorial service/special assembly

Dear [name of parents/carers],

On [date and time] we will be holding a memorial service/special assembly [whichever term is most appropriate] to celebrate the life of your son/daughter, [pupil's name].

As a school community, we will be coming together to share the very unique qualities of [pupil's name] and look at the many wonderful things that they achieved in their life.

We are writing to invite you to join us for this memorial service/assembly [whichever term is most appropriate] and hope that you are able to attend. Please know that if you would like to join us, you can participate to whatever level you are happy with – you are very welcome to play a part in the event or to sit as a member of the audience.

We look forward to hearing from you and if you have any questions or thoughts about the memorial service/special assembly please call me on [telephone number].

I look forward to hearing from you.

Kind regards,

Inviting parents/carers/families and friends of the school to Friendship Day

Dear Parents and Carers,

On [date and time] we will be holding a special Friendship Day at school.

Friendship Day is an annual event where we come together as a school community to celebrate our friends – friends who are with us and friends who have sadly died.

This is a very special and happy day when we think about and cherish our friends. We will think about what makes a good friend and come together for special activities and to play games with each other. There will also be a coffee morning hosted by our wonderful friends in the sixth form [or whichever class it is] with lots of delicious homemade snacks.

As friends of [name of school], we would like you to join us for this special day.

We hope to see you on [date].

Kind regards,

Information to Send Home Following a Death

Listening and showing that you care are the key aspects of supporting a bereaved child.

Death is a subject avoided by most people, especially with children. Most adults are perplexed by what to say to another adult who is mourning, but when a child is bereaved they often try to avoid having a conversation about the loss and try to ignore the issue and all questions about death.

It is our natural instinct to protect children, but trying to protect them from death and the emotions of grief is unwise and unhelpful.

Children who have SEND may communicate their grief differently, but grief is grief, and their grief is just as valid and powerful as anyone else's and must never be overlooked, ignored or forgotten. Doing so will only leave them in a greater state of confusion and, just like anyone whose grief is neglected, this could impact on their emotional and psychological health beyond all measure.

Children want and look for the truth surrounding a death as much as adults. It is crucial that this is given to them (to the level of their developmental understanding).

Key things bereaved children need

- To have their questions answered.
- To be helped to understand about the death.
- To be given the opportunity to be involved, for example in the funeral, memorial service or special assembly at school.
- To be given affection and extra reassurance.
- Opportunities to talk in their own time.
- Opportunities to be left alone.
- To know that they are safe and that there are people who care for them.
- The ability to talk to others (including other professionals) if needed.
- Ways to remember the person.

You will need to be able to communicate the following words and concepts to your child, with symbols, photos, objects of reference and so on (whatever your child's mode of communication is – if you need help with these resources at home, please contact the school):

- dead
- alive (so that you can compare the two and explain what dead and alive mean)
- will not see them again
- sad
- angry
- upset.

You also need to communicate words that explain how and why they died (to the appropriate level of detail for the child and their understanding), such as:

- unwell
- accident
- in hospital
- at home.

Ways to explain death

Below are examples of phrases that you could use when explaining death to a child.

- When a person dies they stop living. A dead person does not breathe, see or hear. They cannot do things. Their body[1] has completely stopped working. The person who has died has gone forever.
- When someone we like dies, we can have many different feelings. We can feel angry, sad and lonely. With time, these feelings start to go away. We are able to learn to live without the person. The person is not forgotten. We remember them and the time we spent together.

---

1   Check that the child understands that the word body means the whole person – the whole body. Often we talk about the head and the body being two separate things so a child may interpret 'their body has completely stopped working' as meaning their head is still OK.

Ways to support a bereaved child

- With the child look at photos and videos of the person who has died. Doing this helps to facilitate and support the child's expression of sadness and anger. As they express these emotions, reinforce what they are feeling and why. Use symbols and all relevant Augmentative and Alternative Communication (AAC) to support this (as below).

  - When they are angry, show them the symbol/picture/sign (whatever their preferred mode of communication is) for 'angry', 'dead', 'OK' and 'miss', along with a photo of the child who has died as you say, 'You are angry because David is dead. It's OK to be angry. You miss David.'

  - When they are crying or sad, follow the same approach. Show them the symbol/picture/sign (whatever their preferred mode of communication is) for 'sad', 'dead', 'OK', 'miss' and 'crying', along with a photo of the child who has died as you say, 'You are sad, because David is dead. It's OK to be sad and crying. You miss David.'

- Read storybooks about death and loss.

- Provide the child with safe activities and opportunities to express their grief (e.g. painting, play dough, using construction kits and physical tasks such as shredding paper or throwing balls). Reassure them that all feelings are OK and acceptable. Expressing their emotions through these activities will be very cathartic for them.

- Having a comforting object to hold can be a great support for children. This object can be whatever is an important and comforting item for the child. It could be a toy, a blanket, a cushion, etc. Having access to this object can help children get through particularly sad and angry times.

Remember to:

- acknowledge your child's grief
- listen to them
- answer their questions
- reassure them that they are safe, loved and cared for.

Please contact the school if you would like any further support.

Lesson Ideas for Activities Following a Bereavement

Creative arts lessons

Following a bereavement, creative arts are a great way for children to express how they are feeling or to be able to get lost in an engaging activity that takes them away from feeling sad about the death (the reaction will depend on the child and how they are feeling at the time of the activity).

Activities that require minimal expertise, but that involve physical engagement and create a project with immense impact, are often best. Here are some examples.

- Splatter painting – give the child/ren a large piece paper, lots of paints and the tool that is easiest for them to hold and make splatter marks with (feather, paintbrush, piece of cloth, etc.). Encourage the child to create marks in whatever manner they wish, the object is to be as expressive as possible.

- Modelling – give the child/ren a piece of clay, play dough, papier-mâché (again, whatever is easiest for them to manipulate or their favourite form of modelling) and just let them mash, bash and express themselves.

- Construction – using the child's preferred construction kit, let them make and explore whatever they are thinking and feeling (for some children a doll's house or role-play corner will be more appropriate and provide a better means of accessing their emotions than construction kits).

- Semi-structured music making – get the child/ren to choose their preferred musical instrument and encourage them to make whatever sounds they feel like; for children who are non-verbal or who have limited communication skills the music will be their words. Move on to providing different soundtracks for the children to accompany – start with angry, sad, upsetting, etc. pieces and move on to more neutral pieces and then peaceful, happy and fun ones. This range of soundtracks will allow the children to explore a range of different emotions. Finish by giving the children the opportunity to play however they feel – this will give you an idea of how they are feeling at the end of the session.

Create a memory board – a display all about the person who has died

Use one of your classroom display boards to create a memory board about the person who has died. If the person was a child and they loved animals, maybe create a farm scene – the child surrounded by their favourite animals. Include other details that are very unique to the child, such as them wearing their favourite colours. Include the children's thoughts and memories about this person on the board too. Get the children to write, draw, cut and stick, add photos and so on (in whatever medium is best for them to communicate their feelings and thoughts) to express what they loved about this person and the special things that they will remember about them.

Emotion baking

Make biscuits with the children (or you can use bought/pre-prepared biscuits) and then give each child three biscuits to decorate. Each child should decorate one biscuit with a happy face, one with a sad face and the final biscuit with a face of their own choosing. Before enjoying the biscuits (eating them!), talk to the children about times when they felt happy and sad and why they felt this way. You can then move on to some of the more complex emotions, as some of the children will have no doubt decorated their third biscuit with an angry face, crying face, tired face, etc., giving you a wide range of emotions related to grief to discuss.

What does dead mean?

Following a death, some children will not understand the finality of death and the fact that these people are unable to 'come back'. Having a sensitive visual representation of what dead means can often help develop this understanding.

Bring two identical plants into the classroom and ensure one is given water and light and the other is completely neglected and given no water. The children will be able to see the neglected plant slowly dying and you can compare what a living plant and a dead plant look like. Once the plant is *completely* dead, get the children to water it and put it in good light, etc. so that they can see that however much they try they are unable to bring it back to life.

This lesson can also be done with two bunches of flowers for a quicker result.

Further Reading

Storybooks

Death of a pupil in a special school

- *Remembering Lucy* by Sarah Helton, Jessica Kingsley Publishers (2017)

General bereavement

- *Always and Forever* by Alan Durant, Corgi (2013)
- *Aunty Mary's Rose* by Douglas Wood, Candlewick Press (2010)
- *Badger's Parting Gifts* by Susan Varley, Picture Lions (2013)
- *Lifetimes* by Bryan Mellonie and Robert Ingpen (1997)
- *Liplap's Wish* by Jonathan London and Sylvia Long, Chronicle Books (1994)
- *Milly's Bug Nut* by Jill Janey, Winston's Wish (2002)
- *My Henry* by Judith Kerr, HarperCollins Children's Books (2011)
- *No Matter What* by Debi Gliori, Bloomsbury (2005)
- *Out of the Blue* (for teenagers) by Winston's Wish, Winston's Wish (2006)
- *The Copper Tree* by Hilary Robinson, Strauss House Productions (2012)
- *When Dinosaurs Die* by Laurie Krasny and Marc Brown, Little Brown Books (1996)

About grief and loss

- *Rabbityness* by Jo Empson, Child's Play (International) Ltd (2012)
- *The Heart and the Bottle* by Oliver Jeffers, HarperCollins (2010)
- *The Lonely Tree* by Nicholas Halliday, Halliday Books (2006)

Death of a mother

- *Missing Mummy* by Rebecca Cobb, Macmillian Children (2012)
- *The Scar* by Charlotte Moundlic, Walker (2013)

Death of a father

- *Princess and the Castle* by Caroline Binch, Red Fox (2016)
- *Samantha's Missing Smile* by Julie Kaplow, Magination Press (2007)

Death of a grandparent
- *Grandad, I'll Always Remember You* by Ann De Bode and Rien Broere, Evans Brothers (1997)
- *Grandpa's Boat* by Michael Catchpool, Andersen Press Ltd (2009)
- *Grandma and Grandpa's Garden* by Neil Griffiths, Red Robin Books (2008)
- *Grandma's Bill* by Martin Waddell, Macdonald Young Books (1991)
- *Ladder to the Moon* by Maya Soetoro-Ng, Walker Books Ltd (2012)
- *Little Bear's Grandad* by Nigel Gray, Little Tiger Press (2000)
- *The Grandad Tree* by Trish Cooke, Walker Books Ltd (2001)

Death of a pet
- *Harry and Hopper* by Margaret Wild, Scholastic (2012)
- *I'll Always Love You* by Hans Wilhelm, Hodder and Stoughton (1985)
- *Sammy in the Sky* by Barbara Walsh, Walker Books Ltd (2012)
- *We Love Them* by Martin Waddell, Walker Books (1990)

Illness and death
- *Gentle Willow* by Joyce C Mills, Magination Press (2003)
- *The Secret C (Straight Talking About Cancer)* by Julie Stokes, Winston's Wish (2009)

Death due to a road accident
- *Someone has Died in a Road Crash* by Mary Williams OBE and Caroline Chisholm, Brake (2006)

Activity/workbooks for children
- *After a Murder: A Workbook for Grieving Kids* by The Dougy Center, The National Center for Grieving Children and Families (2002)
- *Muddles, Puddles and Sunshine: Your Activity Book to Help When Someone Has Died* by Diana Crossley, Hawthorn Press (2000)
- *My Book About Me* by Sally Harrison and Lynda Weiss, Child Bereavement Charity (1996)
- *My Book About Our Baby That Died* by Lynda Weiss, Child Bereavement Trust (1996)
- *Someone I Know Has Died* by Trish Phillips, Child Bereavement Charity (2009)

- *When Someone Very Special Dies: Children Can Learn to Cope with Grief (Drawing out Feelings)* by Marge Heegaard, Woodland Press (1991)

Bereavement resources

- *Blob Bereavement Cards* by Pip Wilson and Ian Long, Speechmark Publishing (2013)
- *Let's Talk About Dying* by Rachel Fearnley, Speechmark Publishing (2012)
- *Memory Garden Bereavement Healing Cards* by Bright Spots Games

Books for adults to help support grieving children

- *A Child's Grief (Supporting a Child When Someone in Their Family Has Died)* by Winston's Wish, Winston's Wish (2009)
- *As Big As It Gets (Supporting a Child when a Parent is Seriously Ill)* by Winston's Wish, Winston's Wish (2007)
- *Beyond the Rough Rock (Supporting a Child Who Has Been Bereaved through Suicide)* by Winston's Wish, Winston's Wish (2008)
- *Hope Beyond the Headlines (Supporting a Child Bereaved Through Murder or Manslaughter)* by Winston's Wish, Winston's Wish (2008)
- *The Family Has Been Informed (Supporting Bereaved Children and Young People From Military Families)* by Winston's Wish, Winston's Wish (2014)
- *You Just Don't Understand (Supporting Bereaved Teenagers)* by Winston's Wish, Winston's Wish (2014)

Information books for professionals

- *A Teacher's Handbook of Death* by Maggie Jackson and Jim Colwell, Jessica Kingsley Publishers (2001)
- *Brief Interventions with Bereaved Children* by Barbara Monroe and Frances Kraus, Oxford University Press (2010)
- *Childhood Bereavement: Developing the Curriculum and Pastoral Support* by Nina Job and Gill Frances, National Children's Bureau (2004)
- *Children and Grief: When a Parent Dies* by J. William Worden, Guilford Press (2002)
- *Coping with Suicide* by Maggie Helen, Sheldon Press (2002)
- *Grief in School Communities* by Louise Rowling, Open University Press (2003)

- *Helping Children with Loss by Margot Sutherland,* Speechmark Publishing Ltd (2003)
- *Loss and Learning Disability* by Noelle Blackman, Worth Publishing (2003)
- *Loss, Change and Bereavement in Palliative Care (Facing Death)* by Pam Firth, Gill Luff and David Oliviere, Open University Press (2004)
- *Loss, Change and Grief: An Educational Perspective* by Erica Brown, David Fulton Publishers (1999)
- *Supporting Young People Coping with Grief, Loss and Death* by Deborah Weymont, Lucky Duck Books (2006)
- *The Forgotten Mourners: Guidelines for Working with Bereaved Children* by Susan C. Smith, Jessica Kingsley Publishers (1999)

Further Information

Child Bereavement Network

www.childhoodbereavementnetwork.org.uk

Child Bereavement Network supports professionals working with bereaved children and young people.

Child Bereavement UK

www.childbereavementuk.org

Child Bereavement UK provides:

- a confidential information and support line for families and professionals when a child has died and when a child is bereaved
- direct support for children and families
- a nationwide database of other local support services
- a web discussion forum for families
- resources for bereaved children and young people, families and all professionals
- training courses on bereavement for health care and other professionals.

Cruse Bereavement Care

www.cruse.org.uk

Cruse provides support after the death of someone close. Many local branches of Cruse offer individual or group support for bereaved children. Cruse also has a special website for young people: www.hopeagain.org.uk.

Cruse Bereavement Care (Scotland)

www.crusescotland.org.uk

Cruse Bereavement Care Scotland helps anyone experiencing bereavement to understand their grief and cope with their loss. Several branches of Cruse Scotland offer support for bereaved children.

Grief Encounter

www.griefencounter.org.uk

Grief Encounter helps bereaved children get help, recognition and understanding following their loss.

Pets as Therapy

www.petsastherapy.org

Pets as Therapy seeks to enhance health and wellbeing in the community through visits of trusted volunteers with their behaviourally assessed animals. It provides a visiting service in hospitals, hospices, nursing and care homes, special needs schools and a variety of other venues all across the UK.

Positive Handling

www.positivehandling.co.uk

Positive Handling helps schools who are dealing with challenging behaviours to effectively and appropriately manage disruptive, risky or extreme situations using appropriate Positive Handling strategies.

PROACT-SCIPr-UK

www.proact-scipr-uk.com

Positive Range of Options to Avoid Crisis and use Therapy – Strategies for Crisis Intervention (revised for the UK) has its roots in the original Strategies for Crisis Intervention and Prevention (SCIP) Programme from the Office of Departmental Disabilities (OMRDD) – State of New York. The programme focused on supporting staff to teach service users to maintain control and to engage in proactive methods of behaviour change.

Rainbows

www.rainbowsgb.org

Rainbows helps children and young people grieve and grow after a loss.

Rescue Remedy

www.bachflower.com / rescue-remedy-information

Rescue Remedy is a blend of five Bach Flower Remedies that are especially beneficial when you find yourself in traumatic and stressful situations.

Sudden

www.suddendeath.org

Sudden supports people after they have experienced a sudden death.

Support after Murder and Manslaughter (SAMM)

www.samm.org.uk

SAMM supports families bereaved by murder and manslaughter.

Survivors of Bereavement by Suicide

www.*uk-sobs.org.uk*

Survivors of Bereavement by Suicide is an organisation offering emotional and practical support for people bereaved through suicide.

Team-Teach

www.teamteach.co.uk

Team-Teach is a positive handling approach that covers risk and restraint reduction, de-escalation techniques and behaviour management.

Victim Support

www.victimsupport.org.uk

Victim Support helps people affected by crime and traumatic events.

Winston's Wish

www.winstonswish.org.uk

Winston's Wish provides:

- a national helpline for all those caring for a child or young person who has been bereaved
- a website with activities for children and young people (plus the facility to ask questions of a trained clinician)
- a programme of direct support for families bereaved through suicide, murder or manslaughter
- resources including books and memory boxes
- training courses and bespoke training.

APPENDIX G

Statistics

Bereavement statistics

Statistics quoted in this book and the following text and bereavement statistics are from: Childhood Bereavement Network (n.d.) *National Statistics.* London: Childhood Bereavement Network. Accessed on 13/01/17 at www.childhoodbereavementnetwork.org.uk/research/key-statistics.aspx.

How many children and young people are bereaved?
Bereavement in children and young people is more frequent than many people think. Seventy-eight per cent of 11–16-year-olds in one survey said that they had been bereaved of a close relative or friend (Harrison and Harrington, 2001).

How many parents die each year, leaving dependent children?
We estimate that in 2015, 23,600 parents died in the UK, leaving dependent children (23,200 in 2014). That's one parent every 22 minutes.

How many children are bereaved of a parent each year?
We estimate that in 2015, these parents left behind around 41,000 dependent children aged 0–17 (40,000 in 2014). That's 112 newly bereaved children every day.

How many children in the current population
have been bereaved of a parent?
By the age of 16, 4.7 per cent or around 1 in 20 young people will have experienced the death of one or both of their parents (Parsons, 2011).

How many children in the current population have
been bereaved of a parent or sibling?
In 2004, the last time a national survey was done, around 3.5 per cent of 5–16-year-olds had been bereaved of a parent or sibling (Fauth, Thompson and Penny, 2009). In today's terms, that equates to around 309,000 school-age children across the UK.

However, as mortality rates have fallen since that survey was carried out, we hope that the rates of bereaved children have also fallen since then. We are joining with others to campaign for the survey to be carried out again, so that we can be more sure of the numbers.

Are some groups more likely to be bereaved?
Yes. Mortality rates vary by social class and geography, so it follows that children living in disadvantaged areas are more likely to be bereaved. Also, some groups of children may be more likely to experience particular kinds of bereavement: for example mortality rates among disabled young people with complex health needs are higher than among the general population, so young people attending special school are probably more likely to be bereaved of a friend than their peers in mainstream schools.

How many schools are supporting bereaved children?
A survey of primary schools in Hull found that over 70 per cent had a child on roll who had been bereaved of someone important to them in the last two years (Holland, 1993). All schools will be affected by bereavement at some point.

References

Department for Education (2016) *SEND: The Schools and Colleges Experience. A Report to the Secretary of State for Education.* London: Department for Education.

Fauth, B., Thompson, M. and Penny, A. (2009) *Associations Between Childhood Bereavement and Children's Background, Experiences and Outcomes: Secondary Analysis of the 2004 Mental Health of Children and Young People in Great Britain Data.* London: National Children's Bureau.

Harrison, L. and Harrington, R. (2001) 'Adolescents' bereavement experiences: Prevalence, association with depressive symptoms, and use of services.' *Journal of Adolescence 24,* 159–169.

Holland, J. (1993) 'Child bereavement in Humberside.' *Educational Research 35,* 3, 289–297.

Intensive Interaction Institute (2016) *What is Intensive Interaction?* Ware: Intensive Interaction Institute. Accessed on 13/01/17 at www.intensiveinteraction.co.uk/about.

Leboyer, F. (1997) *Loving Hands.* New York: Newmarket Press.

Lewis, C. S. (1961) *A Grief Observed.* London: Faber and Faber.

Parsons, S. (2011) *Long-term Impact of Childhood Bereavement: Preliminary Analysis of the 1970 British Cohort Study (BCS70).* London: Child Well-being Research Centre.

Royal College of Psychiatrists (2015) *Bereavement Leaflet.* London. The Royal College of Psychiatrists. Accessed on 13/01/17 at www.rcpsych.ac.uk/healthadvice/problemsdisorders/bereavement.aspx.

Strom, M. (2010) *A Life Worth Breathing.* New York: Skyhorse Publishing.

Worden, W. (2008) *Grief Counseling and Grief Therapy.* New York: Springer Publishing Group.

Index

CPI Antony Rowe
Eastbourne, UK
December 10, 2024